BEAGLE
TALES 2

BY

BOB FORD

ILLUSTRATED BY

ALEXIS MORRISON

BEAGLE TALES 2

FIRST SUNBURY PRESS EDITION
Printed in the United States of America
December 2011

Trade Paperback ISBN: 978-1-934597-94-1
Mobipocket format (Kindle) ISBN: 978-1-934597-95-8
ePub format (Nook) ISBN: 978-1-934597-96-5

Published by:
Sunbury Press
Camp Hill, PA
www.sunburypress.com

Camp Hill, Pennsylvania   USA

From The American Beagler

We were contacted by the publisher of **Beagle Tales**, by Bob Ford about advertising the book in our magazine, *The American Beagler*. Of course, we were interested in running an ad and also requested a copy of the book. After reading the book we contacted Sunbury Press with a message for Bob Ford to contact us to see about the possibility of having him write a monthly article in *The American Beagler*.

We were thrilled when Bob gave us the opportunity to feature him as a writer. We were excited to get a writer of his caliber for a monthly article. We take copies of *Beagle Tales* and the latest issues of *The American Beagler Magazine* with Bob's articles to the Beagle Hunts. We find people laughing and reading the articles out loud.

We are looking forward to Bob's second book.

The American Beagler Magazine
Mike and Janie Ridenhour
PO Box 957
Belle, MO 65013
573-859-6866
www.theamericanbeagler.com
ridenhour000@centurytel.net

FROM
HOUNDS AND HUNTING

We are very pleased to be able to include Bob's writing in *Hounds and Hunting*. His articles bring a fresh, fun approach to the love of beagling.

Our staff anticipates a chuckle with each article, and he never disappoints.

Hounds and Hunting
Since 1903
The Only Magazine Featuring All Types of Beagle Field Trials
www.houndsandhunting.com

Acknowledgments

I would like to thank Bob and Pearl Baker. I faxed them a story ten years ago and they immediately hired me to write for *Better Beagling*, without ever having met me, and started me on the road of writing humor every month! I would also like to thank *The American Beagler* and *Hounds & Hunting*, the two magazines for whom I currently write. My wife, Renee, deserves utmost credit for tolerating my time afield and the bouncing beagles in the house. Lastly, I want to thank Karen for helping me proofread the manuscript. She did not want credit, and so I am obliged not to list her last name. She likes to help people without getting credit. So, I will not list her last name beside her first name. Oh, that reminds me, I need to call her husband about a matter regarding hunting season. His name is Walt Britten.

"Nobody can fully understand the meaning of love unless he's owned a dog. He can show you more honest affection with a flick of his tail than a man can gather through a lifetime of handshakes. I can't think of anything that brings me closer to tears than when my old dog -- completely exhausted after a hard day in the field -- limps away from her nice spot in front of the fire and comes over to where I'm sitting and puts her head in my lap, a paw over my knee, and closes her eyes and goes back to sleep. I don't know what I've done to deserve that kind of friend, but I'm humble enough not to ask any questions."

-- Gene Hill, from the essay "The Dog Man" in a collection of his stories entitled *Tears & Laughter*

ALLERGIES

July is a trade-off for me. The heat is unbearable while on the other hand, we are well into the summer, and so I am out of the cold and flu season. Between shaking hands on Sunday morning with everybody and then going into hospitals and nursing homes the rest of the week, I tend to be susceptible to catching sickness during the winter. This problem has been compounded since getting married and acquiring a stepson. I now have a boy in my house, and as near as I can tell his nose runs all year. This is a long way of saying that I get at least one or two bad colds and/or the flu each winter. However, during the heat of summer this problem evaporates with the heat.

But I am crowding the age of 40. My family doctor is convinced that I must receive the flu shot, because apparently the flu gets worse once you are 40. I explained that I cannot get the flu shot because I am allergic to eggs. The flu vaccine is grown in eggs.

"Oh, any other allergies?" Doc asked.

"Yeah, fish. All seafood. Isn't it in the file?" I asked.

Apparently nothing is in the file, or perhaps the reality is that the file doesn't really get read—it just looks impressive to carry around. This is even more obvious when I go to the doctor and no less than 14 people ask me my name, address, and birthday. At first I thought that this was a preliminary screening for Alzheimer's, but they insist that this is not the case.

"Were you tested for egg allergies?" Doc asked.

"Yep, as a baby. Apparently I ate some scrambled eggs and swelled up like a Macy's Day Parade balloon." I answered.

"Well, we shall see about that," Doc scribbled in my file, "We will have you tested again. Food allergies are commonly outgrown."

My heart leaped with excitement. As a child my vocational plans did not include the ministry. I saw myself as a mountain man. A little research in the 6th grade showed me that mountain men lived off fish in large quantities for much of the year. Ice fishing was important, and spring trout were essential foodstuffs. Allergies, as well as my eyeglasses, seemed to eliminate me from being a mountain man. I could find no pictures of mountain men wearing spectacles. Maybe I could now at least eat trout—I have given thousands away to relatives and friends. Perhaps, with a negative allergy test, I could try them for myself. I could be a mountain man preacher. I could picture it clearly, "Send me to the wilderness Bishop."

A few weeks later I went to the allergist to get tested. He looked at me, my file in his hand, and said "So what are you here for?"

"Isn't it in the file?" I asked.

He stared at me. He looked at the folder, "Umm, sure but why don't you just tell me to make sure that there is no discrepancy." Maybe no doctor can read another's handwriting.

"I am here to get tested for allergies. I am getting close to 40, and apparently that is the age where the flu gets really deadly."

They covered my back with little pins. I almost immediately began to itch with intensity. I mean it felt like my skin was crawling. "Drat!" I thought to myself, only it was another word that started with a "d". I guess trout was still off my diet. Later the results were read to me,

"Well, we will do blood work to confirm, but you are no longer allergic to eggs or fish. Not even shellfish," the doctor said.

"Really, my back is itching everywhere." I said.

"Oh, I know. You are allergic to everything else!" the allergist smiled. I could tell he was planning to make some money. He read the litany of items that are definite allergies, "You are allergic to pretty much all trees, all grass, all the molds except one, ragweed, goldenrod, dust mites, cats, and a little bit to dogs."

"Dogs?" I asked, "I live with beagles."

2

"Better get some air filters. *Hepa* are the best," he handed me a catalog. I was sure he owned stock in the company.

Just this morning I was out running dogs and the pollen seemed to be an inch thick on the truck windshield as I left. I was a little stuffy and sneezed a few times, but otherwise I felt fine. The hounds chased rabbits in a place that contains some trout in a cold stream, and I managed to catch a few for supper. A late morning rain washed the pollen away and I felt less stuffy as the rains fell. I have become a fan of seafood, and eggs are now on the breakfast menu. For years I have watched guys eat breakfast at field trials and thought how good those dippy eggs looked. It was always embarrassing to order my breakfast with no eggs at a field trial. The clubhouse cook always looked at me with disdain. All beagle club cooks fancy themselves as mess hall cooks in the Army, or perhaps a Navy cook in charge of feeding an aircraft carrier. Any special exceptions are looked upon with suspicion. "Whaddya mean no eggs?!" is a common response to such requests. Now when the field trial kitchen asks me how I want my eggs I can say, "However you think is best, Sarge," This works much better than explaining an egg allergy.

I still have beagles in the house. Every so often I will sneeze, but that could just as easily be allergies to trees or grass. Beagles shed like crazy, but if they are in the briars during the morning the hair winds up being combed out by the greenbrier and the multi-floral rose. I have been trying to use my allergy to grass as an excuse to stop mowing it. I figure if I live with a 15-year-old boy, there should never be a reason for me to mow again. Alas, unless there is a video game about mowing lawns, I don't think it will ever happen. It may just be me, but it seems that kids never go outside anymore. I began mowing grass as soon as I could reach the handle. My safety talk from my father was, "Don't you dare mow backwards until I say you're old enough. If you back that mower over your foot and get hurt you will get a spanking as soon as your foot stops bleeding." Such harsh discipline no longer exists. At 15 years of age and nearly six feet in height, all my stepson has to do is tell his mother that he feels that "Mowing damages his self-esteem" and I am out there sniffling and squinting through tears as the grass flies in the air around me.

Even so, I am one step closer to living the dream as a mountain man. I just need to get my eyesight corrected so I can throw away these glasses. I wonder if laser surgery can correct astigmatism. Oh well, even if they do, I will have to carry eye drops into the mountains with me in any month that has trees or grass growing—that seems like a liability when you want to live off the land. Other than that, you can call me Jeremiah Johnson.

It was nearing the Fourth of July, and I was about to have a celebration. We would thaw the last of the rabbits from the freezer and defrost some venison and trout. We were going to have a wild game feast to celebrate Independence Day. If I couldn't be a mountain man, I would at least have some wild game for the holiday. The very wet spring produced lots of wild mushrooms that I dehydrated. They would go well with the venison steaks. I was also going to try my first deviled eggs. I wanted to say thank you to all the troops serving around the world. My prayer was that you would all be home safe, very soon. You let me dream of being a mountain man while I ran beagles every morning.

FATHER'S DAY

I was never able to sleep in late, not even as a teenager. In the summer, my friends would sleep until 10:00 a.m. or later, and I would be bored awaiting their arrival to play baseball or some other game. And then I got beagles. I saved my tip money from delivering the Erie Sunday Times, and in June of 1985, not long after Father's Day, we drove to Erie, PA and I bought Duke as an 8-week-old puppy for $75.00. My sister thought the puppies were cute and Dad bought another pup from a different litter for the same price. Princess was to be jointly owned by my father and sister. My sister and I were to take turns cleaning the wire run kennel that Dad built, but my sister never took her turn with the wire brush and hoe! Every day I scrubbed the wire with a toilet brush that I dipped into the largest sized metal coffee can sold in the grocery store filled with water and pine-scented cleaner. To this day, I can't smell pine-based cleaning agents without associating it with the hind end of beagles.

Sis said that her half of Princess did the eating and she wasn't cleaning the kennel. Funny, she never fed the dogs either, which is the chore that would have gone with the half that she owned. It was Dad and I that took care of the dogs. We were in the woods every morning except when Dad was working from 7-3. On those weeks we hit the briars in the evening. It was wonderful to have my mornings filled with the sounds of hounds. Those beagles got accustomed to running every morning, and they would erupt with howls whenever they thought we were going to the field. I remember coming downstairs to see Dad smoking his pipe in the darkened kitchen.

"Don't turn on that light," He said as I entered the kitchen, "Eat your cereal in the dark." Dad sipped his coffee. Sure enough, the beagles had learned to anticipate the morning runs by noticing the houselights. "Sneak a

5

peek out the window," Father said. At this point I wondered if we were training dogs or if they were training us.

I sneaked to the window curtain. Duke and Princess were standing at attention, looking out the kennel towards the house, cocking their heads to the side and straining to hear any hints that we were about to load them into the truck that they believed they owned. The entire goal was to load the hounds as quickly as possible so as to minimize the noise that the neighbors had to endure as the duo howled in anticipatory delight of the chase to come. This was how Dad and I spent summers for the first few years of my beagling life, until I turned 16 and could get a summer job (other than mowing lawns and splitting firewood). We had breakfast in the dark, and then made a dash for the truck. I still get up early every morning. Dad never lived long enough to see me graduate college or seminary, and I often wonder if he would be surprised that I still have beagles. I know he would be surprised that they live in the house. As United Methodist clergy, I get moved occasionally, and building a kennel would be a waste of money. So I have a few hounds, and run them all hard, like when I was a kid. I got in the habit of feeding beagles in the morning except on the days I am taking them afield. When we head to the briars they skip the morning feeding and will eat after we chase the daily rabbits. Either way, they are awake before dawn looking to eat kibbles or rabbit tracks. I still wonder if I am training beagles or if they are training me. My mother got to sleep while Dad and I sat in the dark whispering over coffee and cereal. My wife, on the other hand, hears the hounds as they demand that I give them the morning exercise that has become standard in our home. Dad felt that all children should have as much fun as possible and all the responsibility that they could shoulder. He let me stay in the woods as long as I wanted, and only gave me a curfew if I went into town. I still think through my big decisions while listening to hounds sing. Every Father's Day I give thanks for a Dad that gave me the gift of beagling. And thanks to all of you beaglers out there that share our sport with kids. I would clap my hands for you, but it is early in the morning and I am typing in the dark hoping the hounds do not hear the keyboard—it is raining really hard and I do not want to go to the woods today.

ORANGE GATE ROAD

I have two hunting stories that are very much related. First, there is the event a few deer seasons ago. The event happened in the late afternoon, just before dark. My friend Lee and I were on our way out of the woods when a deer emerged from the tree line at the top of a field. I sat down and rested my Colt .30-06 on my knees and scoped the whitetail. "It's a doe," I said.

"You have a doe tag?" Lee asked.

"Yeah, two of 'em" I replied. "It looks pretty far though."

"Ah, go ahead. You can do it," came his response.

We were very close to one of our favorite rabbit hunting spots. I see myself as a rabbit hunter, and I really hunt deer to lower their population in places where I do not want my beagles tempted to run the wrong game. A deep breath and a slow squeeze were followed by the crack of the gun.

"You got it," Lee said. "Let's go get her."

The recoil settled and I looked through the scope, "I missed, I see her running to the left."

"Different deer," Lee assured me, "I think it was bedded down and ran after your shot. I saw the deer fall." As we neared, the deer got bigger. I was amazed at the size compared to what I saw through the scope. Later, it was ranged at nearly 300 yards.

The next story happened during small game season, just a few hundred yards away from the location of the previously mentioned marksmanship. I was waiting as a rabbit streaked down a path straight at me. BLAM! BLAM! I used both barrels of my shotgun and the rabbit ran past me close enough I could have clubbed it with my A.H. Fox 16 gauge. Soon the beagles emerged and the chase continued for another circle. This time the rabbit gave me a broad side shot. BAM! The rabbit kept running and was in the thickets before I could use the other trigger. The chase

8

thundered up the hill towards some greenbrier and I heard Lee shoot. He came down with the rabbit, dogs dancing behind him, and we moved on to new cover to jump another rabbit.

Now, I am not saying that I always miss rabbits three times, and I also would never say that I can make every 300 yard rifle shot. What I am saying is that I was taught to aim a rifle at a young age and had lots of practice, and my self-taught shotgun skills mean that my rabbit success is due to the dogs, not me. I was in my late twenties before a skilled shot-gunner taught me that I should not aim a shotgun. Years later, I am still re-educating myself to shoot a shotgun. Where did I learn to shoot?

There was an orange pipe gate blocking a dirt road not too far from where I grew up. Beginning when I was eight years old, we would park at the gate and walk down the dirt road until we reached a little opening. Dad would put the target down, and then I would shoot a box of .22 shells through a single shot bolt action .22. We began with a big coffee can—you know the biggest sized tin can of coffee that they used to make? Slowly we moved down in size to the one pound coffee can. It was always *Maxwell House* or *Hills Brothers*, which ever was the cheapest. Nowadays, coffee cans are plastic, but those tin cans were everywhere when I was a kid. There was a cabinet filled with the small coffee cans in our basement. Each one was designated for different sized nails, screws, and bolts.

Coffee was everywhere in my childhood. People would drop by the house all the time, and a pot was immediately brewed. This was an era when T.V. only had PBS, CBS, NBC, and ABC. People were looking for reasons to not watch television. More than that, photographs were developed from film then and in rural Pennsylvania we did not have a one-hour development option. So, whenever someone got pictures of a prize buck, opening day of trout season, Christmas morning, a graduation ceremony, wedding, or a family reunion, it was a big deal. It may have been a week since the owner turned in the film at the drugstore. The pictures were not digital. There was no easy way to send the choice photos in an instant to everyone you knew. No Facebook or text messaging. This meant that people would actually have physical interaction with one another (To any teenager reading this: people actually talked face to face then-for real). Relatives and neighbors were constantly dropping in to visit, and it seemed that coffee could be smelled all day long as hospitality was extended. I remember cookies and pies being made from scratch in the late evening or early morning hours in order to stockpile enough snacks to accompany the coffee that was automatically given to the arriving company.

And week after week, Dad and I took a coffee can into the woods and filled it with holes. We always brought the can home for the garbage. When I could hit the can 50 times in a row (an entire box) we moved to a smaller can. I was shooting open sights at 40 yards or so, and I relished the time away from entertaining relatives and friends on Sunday afternoons. Eventually, we ran out of cans. That seems hard to imagine, given the gallons of coffee that seemed to be consumed daily, but it really happened. The consolation was that by the time we ran out of cans (we even used Dad's nail cans and built a new storage facility) I was able to hit the smallest can every time. But we needed a new target.

I remember many heated conversations between my Uncle Tom and my father in the kitchen. They seemed to hold different opinions on just about everything. To be honest, I am not sure why they talked so frequently! Tom was retired and had worked at the same factory where Dad still earned his pay. He knew the rigors of changing shifts every week and the odd sleep schedule that accompanies such weekly changes. In fact, Tom knew the schedule so well that he always seemed to arrive when Dad was home. My father felt that perhaps Tom had no friends. Dad and his brother were having an argument-conversation on a Sunday afternoon, and I was anxious because it was time for us to go shoot. I feared that Tom would not let us get out the door. My uncle always had a dip of *Copenhagen* snuff in his lip and periodically he would go outside, spit, and return to the conversation. On that day, he went to add a pinch of snuff and threw an empty can in the garbage as he produced his *Case* pocketknife to slice the paper that sealed the lid on the new can. We lived fairly close to Bradford, Pennsylvania, so almost everyone carried a *Case* pocketknife. Dad stopped the conversation and ran to the garbage. He reached in and produced the empty snuff can and faced the shiny metallic lid towards me. "Go get your gun and shells," he said to me.

Uncle Tom could have emptied a target every day if we needed it. He definitely enabled us to shoot once each week and sometimes we would go twice. Out to that orange pipe gate we would go, and then walk back to one safe spot or another to shoot. At first the target seemed impossible, but I learned to hit it. I slowed down my shooting, which was not hard since I had fired the gun so often that the ejector no longer worked. I sat on the ground cross-legged with each foot under the opposite leg, and I raised my knees to provide a stable platform just as Dad had taught me. Dad said that this was better than prone because you could see through the brush better. My father's *Case* knife lay on the ground beside me, small blade opened. In between shots, I would slowly open the bolt. The ejectors would pull the cartridge out halfway before they lost grip. At the halfway point, I would grab Dad's knife and flick the brass the rest of the way out of the action. The already slow single shot became even slower. No matter, I was having a ball. Soon I could hit the snuffbox with almost every shot.

The coffee cans could be replenished. The large cans made perfect berry buckets. Poke two holes opposite each other near the top and tie a clothesline for a strap and a perfect berry bucket emerged. Lots of berries were to be found along that road. Sometimes, I would ride my bicycle there and pick them. Teaberries, June berries, blueberries, strawberries, and blackberries could all be found in their season. These sweet fruits were highly sought to bake muffins that would accompany the massive quantities of coffee going out the door. Soon I learned that our neighbors would pay me for those berries in order to bake the desserts needed to host their own company. I began selling to them, until Gram found out and insisted that I give her all my forest fruits. She matched their price. By this time I was old enough to hunt. The orange gate road was where my Dad always hunted deer, but in the berry season I found lots of rabbits. I mean lots, and I made a mental note of this for the upcoming season.

Our beagles found the berry patch rabbits right away, and I was scared from the start by the chase. They were almost out of hearing when I asked Dad, "Is that a deer? The circle seems too big for a rabbit."

Dad squinted and cocked his ear to the side. Decades of work in a loud factory had robbed his hearing, "Can you hear the dogs?" he asked.

"Barely," I replied.

"Getting louder or more silent?" he asked

"Maybe louder, but they are way out there," I answered, cocking my ear like him to try and gauge the truth of the matter. "Definitely getting louder now," I confirmed.

"O.K. Get a spot," Dad answered.

The rabbit made several large circles before it came close enough for a shot. I had a cheap bolt action *Western Auto* 20 gauge shotgun that I bought with paper route tips. The rabbit was way in front of the dogs and stood still to look over his shoulder. One shot and it was over. I walked over to get the rabbit. "Dad, it doesn't even look full grown!" I said.

He came over and puffed on his pipe, grabbing the rabbit as apple scented smoke filled the air. The autumn bugs scampered away. "Woods rabbit," he said through teeth that clenched his pipe," "He is full grown. Woods rabbits run farther circles too." We shot a lot of rabbits there over the years, and all of them looked a little small, and ran massive circles almost out of hearing—you know those big squared off circles with few checks? One day after Christmas, we were walking out of the woods with the dogs on leashes after a long hunt. Dad stopped and pointed at the biggest rabbit tracks I ever saw. The tracks were leading under some hemlock. "Snowshoe," Dad said, "You too tired to run if we have to?"

"No, why?"

"This thing might cross the hardtop road if it is pushed." He unleashed Princess and I unleashed Duke. Soon I saw a flash of white as the hare leaped out of the hemlocks. The dogs were off! They moved away from the hardtop on a circle that was smaller than the woods rabbit.

But the second circle was way out of hearing. We picked the dogs up near dark and never did see that hare again that day, but we knew where to find him later.

I now know that a woods rabbit is a subspecies of the cottontail. It is sometimes called the New England cottontail, but also goes by the handle of Allegheny rabbit or Appalachian cottontail. If you are fond of Latin, the taxonomic name is *Sylvilagus obscurus.* They are slightly smaller, never have white on the forehead, and often have a black spot between the ears. A black rim is very commonly found along the edge of the ears. They are the only cottontail that eats conifer needles. Biologists say that you need to measure the skull to verify the Allegheny rabbit from the Eastern cottontail, but I feel I can differentiate them by the chase. If the rabbit goes out into heavy timber in big circles and returns to cover that looks good for deer, I tend to guess Appalachian Cottontail. *Sylvilagus obscurus* is rare, they say. Snowshoe hare are increasingly uncommon in Pennsylvania as well. When I was a child, a hunter was permitted to harvest two per day for the short season. Now, only one hare can be killed each day of the still very short season.

Today, the Orange Gate Road is closed to the public. Generations of hunters are no longer allowed to go back there. There are Marcellus Shale gas wells back there now, and no one can enter unless they check in at the little trailer-style building where I.D. is verified. Marcellus Shale drilling is controversial in the Keystone State. Clean water, and the threat to it, lies at the core of the debate. Massive amounts of natural gas profits are also involved. I look down a road that leads to the woods that I grew up wandering, and I am forbidden to enter. I learned to hit deer at long range (easier than a snuff can at 40 yards) in those woods. Two rare game species live there—the Appalachian cottontail and the varying hare. Sure, I respect private property and public lands for hunting are becoming a thing of the past—I get it. Still, a part of me mourns the loss of that past. I ain't a politician, and Lord knows I can't make any changes. In the words of Lynyrd Skynyrd "All I can do is write about it..." That is a great song. If you want, I will bring the song to your house and we can have coffee- providing you like Southern Rock. Of course, you could also find the song on YouTube.

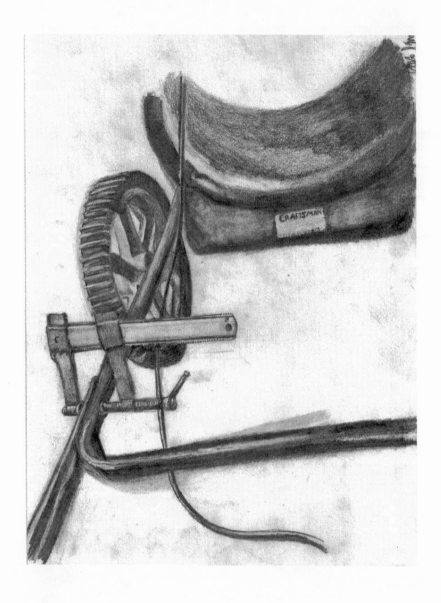

TOOLS

I was having breakfast with the guys when the topic of lawn care leaped into the conversation. "I like my grass cut nice and low, in case I get rained out for a few days," Lenny said

"Three inches. I keep it at three inches," Mert, a retired guy, commented, "I mow it every three days to keep it that height, and I have eliminated the weeds so I can walk barefoot through the thick, soft grass."

And so the conversation rattled, with talk about rolling the lawn, feeding it, hatred for dandelions, and all the rest. Naturally, there were comparisons of lawn care equipment, debates on fertilizer, extended talk of various grass species and more.

"Ford, you got a zero turn mower or a small yard tractor?" Blaine asked, as if everyone owned one or the other.

"Neither," I replied, "I have an old push mower. I spent my money on beagles and shotguns and went with the cheap lawn care."

"Do you sharpen the blade to get a level cut?" Jack asked.

"Every month or so," I said.

"That's too often!" Howard blurted. "You will wear it out."

"There is a rock that protrudes just a bit up from the ground," I explained, "I hit it about every month. That is the only sharpening it gets." My comment sent cold chills down the spines of the lawn care fanatics. In order to save them from nightmares, I decided not to share with them the fact that the engine never gets the oil changed, and a C clamp holds the handle together. They wouldn't understand.

It isn't the first time that my neglect of these sorts of tools has horrified my friends. Not long ago Lenny was fixing my truck. "Got a 10mm deep well socket?" He asked from under the vehicle.

"Sure do," I groaned as I strained to haul a five gallon bucket of sockets and wrenches to his side. The little things never stay in the slots of the boxes they come in, some sockets would get lost and I always had to look for certain sized sockets in one tool kit and other sizes in another. So I dumped all the little buggers into one bucket. I threw the wrenches on top—sort of the stone soup of hand tools. There might even be a stone in that bucket. Lenny, a master shade tree mechanic, almost cried when he looked in the white plastic bucket that once held drywall mud.

"You poor babies..." he sobbed over the tools the way that most of us do when we see footage of children stricken with famine. His sobbing only got louder when he saw the words "TOOL BOX" written on the side of the bucket. When he finished repairing the vehicle I put the lid back on the bucket and returned it to the corner of the garage between the bucket that said "Nuts, Bolts & Washers" and another that read "Sidewalk Salt".

"Those tools deserve better treatment than salt gets!" Lenny bawled as he went home after the job.

I am sure they do. When I was young I dreamed of building beautiful wooden creations like my father would do on a regular basis. His workshop routinely produced desks, cabinets, shelves, odds and ends, cabinets, or whatever. He built entire houses. In my hands the same tools may as well be a stone-age axe as I bash my way through the job. Sure, I can, on occasion, make something structurally sound, but it is always ugly. I have such a reputation for construction incompetence that whenever I repair something my wife says that "Good Enough Construction" is on the job. That is the name of my company, in her opinion. This business name was born out of an attempt I made to fix a cabinet that was having hinge problems.

"How is that?" I beamed with pride after the repairs were finished.

She looked dejected as she noticed the discoloration of the wood where I had to use larger screws from the bolt bucket in the garage. She also noticed that I had to move the hinges in such a way that they no longer lined up at the same height as all the other cabinets. "It is...good enough," She sighed in resignation. Thus, Good Enough Construction was born. Evidence of Good Enough Construction can be found everywhere—my raised garden beds, the bookshelves, a picnic table, and a workbench.

Speaking of raised garden beds, my yard tools aren't treated any better. I have good crops, but I do not treat my shovels, rakes, and hoes with anywhere near the respect that such tools deserve. I leave trowels stuck in the vegetable beds year-round. Shovels lean against a tree for weeks at a time. Real gardeners avert their eyes when in my yard.

The list of tools that I have to borrow is endless. I have only the most basic equipment. I don't even have a single pipe wrench. One bad experience with plumbing has convinced me to find the main shut-off valve to the house for any plumbing complication and simply close it until someone arrives. I live in a church owned house, and I serve a flock that has plenty of talented people and they are astonished at how few tools I own. No table saw, no band saw, no planer. I have no power tools except a drill, a circular saw, and lawn care thing that is designed to safely cut small tree limbs . . . we use it to cut the hooves from deer that we butcher.

Do I have a snow blower? Nope, I use a shovel. In fact, it is my great regret that they no longer make those wonderful, heavy snow shovels that could double as an ice chopper. They were monstrous and weighed so much that you couldn't even notice the additional mass of a shovel full of wet snow, but they were my kind of blunt tool.

Ah, but, there is another side to me. In my mind, those items are all implements for chores. A chore implement is not a tool. There are many things I do not own. I will give you a partial list: lawn tractor, sidewalk edger, leaf blower, snow blower, chain saw, sewer snake, rotor tiller, power washer, trailer, welder, scroll saw, router, drill press, and air compressor. Don't feel bad for me—those are all things easily borrowed. More importantly, I have saved money enough to buy good hunting equipment. Those items are my tools, and I take really good care of them.

I have double barreled shotguns that are vintage, American made firearms. An A.H. Fox 16 gauge is my favorite. It is in perfect condition and is cleaned regularly, as are the other guns. There are tracking collars that receive better maintenance than most vehicles. I have bells, nice ones (made in Canada and purchased from Lion Country Supply) that can be heard a long ways. These are vital to the safety of my dogs when the fall fields are full of thick brush and city-slickers that shoot at moving vegetation. These bells are cleaned and stored neatly.

Boots? I got boots! Heavy warm boots for winter, light leather boots for dry fall days. A strong pair of rubber boots for the morning dew. I even have waterproof sneakers for easy running at the beagle club. They all stand at attention by the door between the basement and the garage, awaiting marching orders as the seasons move through the cycles. Beside the boots, hanging on the wall, is a pair of snowshoes. Alongside the snowshoes is a pair of slip-on cleats for those second season days when an afternoon thaw is followed by a late night freeze that makes for slippery morning hunts.

I hesitate to even tell you about hunting clothes, for fear my wife will read this article and realize just what I do have and insist that she go clothes shopping. I use nothing but Filson vests and pants. Yeah, they are expensive, but you only purchase those things once, because they last forever. They form my outer armor against briars. I have layers of various pants and shirts for underneath the thick Filson canvas. Some layers are cotton and some are wool. There are hi-tech things I can't pronounce. Socks exist for every temperature and precipitation. There is a chest of drawers just for hunting clothes.

And I change guns based on the weather. Ever hold a nice shotgun that that seems way too short in the store? It fits just right with all those layers of winter coats on a December hunt. When tall grass and thick goldenrod prevent me from seeing into that October cover, I carry a small, light gun that lets me maneuver better. After the hard frosts and snowstorms obliterate the weaker plants, opening up long-range shots, I use a gun that reaches out a bit further.

My buddies laugh at my tools. But I laugh at theirs, too. Nothing funnier than a guy in the woods with cold, wet feet on the snow shooting an auto-loading shotgun that is way too long with his winter coat's bulk. He can't figure out why he misses all the time. The barrel is rusted because instead of cleaning the fine tool after he gets home from the snow and rain, he is in a hurry to blow the leaves off the sidewalk. He probably has his hunting clothes in a 5-gallon bucket or a garbage bag in a closet. I guess we all have a different opinion about what makes a fine tool. Now, if you will excuse me, I have to try and borrow a weed trimmer for that last cut of the year.

KIDS' TABLE

Beaglers are a strange group, and this is most clearly seen in the fanatical devotion we have for our favorite brag hounds and our inability to tolerate any disparaging comments about those beagles. And yet the same beaglers seem to have little protective instincts for people. Take the following conversation, which I overheard at a field trial many years ago.

"I thought I heard someone in town say your oldest boy got in trouble over the weekend," said a man we will call Ralph.

"Yep," said Jim, "You know Junior has always had a temper. He got caught, and that is the way it is."

"Yeah, I guess he was never much of a person to get along with anyone. He even quit school cuz he couldn't be polite with the teachers, didn't he?" Ralph nodded his head while he asked as if answering his own question

"You got that right," Jim nodded his head even more as if to signify that he was verifying Jim's memory.

"Guess he won't be able to amount to much with no high school degree and a police record."

"I reckon you're right," Jim answered, "That's my boy."

This whole conversation occurred as we were waiting to run dogs in the next trio. It was a class of 30+ at a gundog brace trial, the judges decided to go with trios. My dog was going to run next against hounds owned by Jim and Ralph. Soon we went into the brush and cast our dogs. A cottontail jumped almost immediately by Ralph's dog. The trio roared over the hill and made a full circle rather quickly. The dogs then sped off in another circle. We remained behind the hounds so as to not affect the path of the rabbit. Jim was ordered to pick up his dog and Ralph and I finished the trio with our hounds running. On the way out of the running grounds, the two friends picked up their conversation where it had left off before we cast our dogs.

"Well," said Ralph, "That was a shame about your son."

"Yep."

"Hey, what did the judge pick your dog up for?" Ralph asked.

"Backtracking," Jim answered, "Can you believe that?"

"Well," Ralph said as he chewed on a plug of tobacco, "We couldn't see much of the chase, but your dog does backtrack one in a while."

"What did you say?" Jim growled, "That's a damn lie and you know it! I oughtta rip your head off!"

The two friends wandered off towards the club kennels very upset with each other. I sat amazed that Jim would tolerate any number of insults directed at his son, but was ready to fight about the performance of a beagle in a field trial. That can, unfortunately, be a big part of beagling. I suppose that there are many beaglers hoping to get a field champion that out performs all others, a stud that produces legions of little field champions and puts the proud owner's kennel on the map. Just as such conflicts erupt between individual beagle owners at individual trials, so too it occurs amongst advocates of various formats and federations.

I live in Pennsylvania, and the conflict between gundog trials and traditional brace is very real. When I was a kid, I belonged to a traditional brace club. There were no SPO trials then. The brace guys only rarely ran dogs, and my father and I almost always had the running grounds to ourselves at our beagle club. In return I was sent to work the field trials (traditional brace) by participating in a skirmish line of armed men swinging sticks in the brush to push rabbits out to the dogs. I would be ordered into the thickest cover to push cottontails, and I returned home with a lot less blood in my body from all those briars. I ran dogs at our club every non-hunting day that there was no trial, and therefore I was often consulted by the field-marshal for information about good cover within our running grounds.

I did get in trouble once when rabbits were scarce during second series. After walking for quite some time without locating a rabbit, a judge watched me crawl through some briars and asked, "Well, how do you think we should find the next rabbit?"

"If someone here drove me home I could get one of my beagles and we could save ourselves some pain," I said, "We just let the dogs find 'em." I realize now that this was insulting to the traditional brace crowd, but I was genuinely trying to be helpful. Don't get me wrong, I still believe that dogs should be able to find rabbits, but I don't understand the animosity amongst beaglers. Oh, and I say that as a guy who has had the slow dogs in the brush!

There was a time when I was a member at Corning Beagle Club when my dogs were on the more conservative end of the spectrum. There were some seriously fast dogs at the club, and my medium speed stuff was maligned. Discussions of speed have often gotten me in hot water. One cool summer evening at the beagle club I once remarked, "As a hunter, I want a fast dog."

"Then why dontchya own any?" laughed a friend.

"I do," I answered, "I measure the speed of a dog in terms of minutes per circle, not miles per hour on a mowed feed strip." I explained that I believed great foot with lots of breakdowns was not what I wanted, but that there was no such thing as too much foot if it was done with good checks work and accuracy. Everyone, the advocates of really quick hounds and the guys that like more style was mad at me for that comment. I guess I want my cake and I want to eat it too. Here are two statements that I have heard other guys say, and I agree with both.

A guy once said to me, "Large Pack trials are the most fair because all of the dogs have the same scenting conditions." Large pack hounds are often seen as the fastest style, as the entire class is cast at once.

A gundog brace trialer maintained, "A brace format is the best way to find the best dog on that day. A dog that can't solve a check cannot hide in a brace the way it does in a pack." Gundog brace is often viewed as the format with the most line control (aside from the traditional brace!).

I suppose I agree with both of those houndsmen, and I know that they would never agree with one another. I have seen winners' packs with dogs unable to solve checks because they were able to hide in the pack. That seems especially easy to do with inexperienced judges. And who doesn't want to be the first pack or brace on the ground when the morning dew makes scent strong? Beaglers have strong opinions. But that is good practice for other things that we have to do in life.

For instance, look at Thanksgiving. Whenever large families gather, there is bound to be some explosive conversations. Why is it that the dynamics of family feasts always find a way of putting people of opposite political views next to each other? The fireworks may even begin before the meal is eaten, at least if you have more than one "expert" trying to cook the same turkey. I once watched my grandmother, mother, and two aunts try to cook the same bird behind the backs of the other women. Each would sneak into the kitchen when the others were not there and open the oven door and shake some seasoning or pour some marinade. Then each matriarch would also close the oven door. Any witnesses would be ordered to silence as the clandestine cook placed an index finger on her nose with a "Shh" sound.

And then the meal is served. "Could you pass the turkey?" is answered with "Is it free range organic?" The teetotaler sits across from the uncle who has been drinking a beer before the meal is served. Grandma always insists that store bought piecrust is not as good as homemade, which makes her own daughter furious because she made the pie with store bought ingredients. Somebody will be a Dallas Cowboys fan (an endangered species in Steelers' Country) and insist that the game be turned on while we eat. No one will turn the game on. There are always way more children than there are turkey legs. At least two people will be assigned to the "kids table" and disagree with that decision.

The kids table is actually where I will volunteer to sit in order to find some sanity. I am often told to remedy the drumstick dispute.

"O.K." I once joked, "You guys wanna fight until only two of you are left standing? Those two get the legs."

The kids started sizing each other up for the grudge match. They did not get the joke. I then arrived at a more equitable decision, "Two of you get the drumsticks, and the other two can have the wishbone later to make a wish."

"What about me?" a fifth child cried.

"If you stop crying, I will eat your cranberries and give you my pumpkin pie. It is really good pie, but if I don't eat it, then I won't have to tell grandma how good it is. You can tell her. Then you will have something to cry about."

After the drumstick dilemma is settled, the conversation is much more pleasant at the kids' table. They disagree about everything, but they still like each other. Favorite colors, toughest superheroes, meanest school teachers, and ways to hide vegetables are all disputed, but no one really fights or cares if the other children feel differently. Come to think of it, aren't we always saying that we need more kids in our sport?

PAPERWORK

I had just finished supper when the telephone rang. It was in the era before caller I.D., so I had no idea who was contacting me. I feel a bit of nostalgia for those days, to be honest. Nowadays, when a free-loading relative calls for a favor, you can see the person's name on the screen and brace yourself for the inevitable. Similarly, if a childhood friend who has relocated several states away rings, you can readily determine that information. This particular phone call, like all phone calls at that time, was a mystery.

"Hello?" I answered.

"Hey Bob, it's Jack."

Jack was the funeral director in the town where I lived, and although clergy and funeral directors have a great working relationship, I think it is safe to say that pastors tend to not care if we hear much from our work colleagues —they tend to carry bad news. My heart sank as I awaited the name of the recently deceased, "Hi, Jack," was all I could muster.

"Want to do some paperwork tomorrow?" He asked.

"Sure!" my crestfallen mood instantly changed to exhilaration, "What time?"

"Oh, how about eight o'clock tomorrow morning?" he suggested.

"I will be there."

Anyone who knows me is aware of the fact that the only thing I like less than meetings is paperwork. In this case, however, "paperwork" was code for "go hunting pheasants down by the lake." It also happens to be a great thing to tell people you are doing and no one will come be a spectator as you fill out forms. I always feel bad for people that have jobs where they do really interesting things. You know, like if you talk to a logger and ask, "What are you doing tomorrow?" Perhaps the logger responds by saying, "Well, I am going to cut down that tree at the old Johnson

25

place, the limbs are growing all through the electrical lines and two big one are dangling above the roof of the house." You can bet that people are going to go watch that tree get cut, just because of the potential for excitement.

When you do paperwork, there are no fans. I have never had anyone sit across the desk from me with bug-eyed wonder as I open envelopes, fill out questionnaires, enter data, or prepare documents to be mailed. If I do homework at home, the beagles won't even hang around; unless I make a snack, and then they will suddenly appear at the sound of rustling bread bags or the popping sound of the refrigerator seal as the door opens.

Several times each year Jack and I would do paperwork along the lake where the pheasants were stocked by the game commission. In fact, they had been stocked for enough consecutive years that there was a locally breeding population that had managed to sustain itself in that part of northern Pennsylvania. The birds tend to winter better in the southern part of the state, but we had some hardy survivors, as evidenced by the occasional sighting of a hen with her young walking across springtime roads. Such sightings were rare, but they did happen. There were, however, lots of stocked birds as well. These are not the smartest animals, and even without a dog you could walk along and get a few. I had borrowed a 12 gauge just for those birds, as my 16 never seemed to do as well as I would like. The pheasant would plop to the ground and then run like a rabbit when I used my Ithaca 16 gauge pump. The borrowed 12 gauge was much more efficient. I now own a couple 12 bores.

Contrary to popular opinion, pastors do work more than on Sunday mornings. I once had a parishioner shadow me for a few days because he thought the sight of my vehicle at a briar patch in the morning meant that I wasn't working. Evidently he was unaware that I was writing my sermon as the dogs chased. He accepted my invitation to work with me for a few days and he was a little late for our pre-arranged 6 a.m. rabbit chasing rendezvous. I produced a tablet and Bible. He seemed offended when I asked what scriptural passage he was utilizing to write his message although, in his defense, he

26

may have been more sleepy than offended. Following the morning chase, we returned hounds to the house and embarked upon the visits to the sick parishioners. After three days of following me, he got tired of eating cafeteria food in the hospitals and drinking coffee during late evening meetings to stay awake. He decided that running dogs at dawn wasn't fun if he had to work the rest of the day.

But "paperwork" is different. It is hunting—no sermon prep. I feel no guilt about hunting a few hours in the morning before work during the rabbit season. Not every morning, mind you: some days I may leave the house before dawn to do hospital visits several hours away at a facility with better equipment and physicians and not get to hunt at sun rise. On those days of hunting season, I might return from the hospital calls and sneak into the brush for the last couple hours of daylight for a quick hunt between the pastoral visits of the day and the meetings of the evening. I have been known to show up for Bible study wearing brush pants and boots.

"Paperwork" is what renews me, and as I type this column, I can feel that the air is getting a little crisper and the first day of the season is within sight. All those hours of chasing professional rabbits inside the beagle club during the summer will soon make my beagles look spectacular. The chases in hunting season are on rabbits that very seldom double, and tend to run big circles with few checks. The same pack that sounds great inside the fence on a summer evening will sound incredible on wet autumn dew as they run after wild rabbits that may never have encountered a beagle.

The season is still weeks away, and I am already transferring things into my truck. Boots, leashes, some shotgun shells, hunting vests, orange hats (I am forever losing orange hats), little brush shears, extra pocketknives, collapsible water bowls to carry afield, and other little items that will be needed for the hunt. The dogs sense it too. The old veterans feel the morning chill and are getting restless. I tend to not run them very much in the summer because the heat seems to be harder on an old dog. But recent weeks have provided some great workouts for the old timers. Often, I only get to hunt two hours at a time, and a seasoned veteran can get a daily limit of four rabbits in that short span. He is just as tired after those two hours as he was after three times as much chasing when he was young, but the results are the same. Those old dogs still strut around the living room and curl up next to the fireplace just as they did before the grey hairs invaded their black blanketed backs.

The young dogs are eager as well, and although they haven't the same experience, they too seem to be aware that the season is close at hand. They are stronger and fitter at this point, and will be the heart and soul of those all day Saturday hunts. One young hound of promise is gaining ground on the veterans with rapid pace, and is getting her fair share of the checks. Her solo time in the brush throughout the summer has really brought out her ability. Lastly, it is time to do a little clay pigeon shooting to sharpen the reflexes before the opening day. Yes, the last minute things will be done a week or more before the last minute. It is time to hunt. I hope you are swamped in "paperwork."

A BEAGLER'S DICTIONARY

I have been writing beagle stories for almost ten years, and over that time I continue to be frustrated by the number of beagle specific terms that my word processor does not recognize. As in many things, I think that there exists a prejudice where the bird dog community gets favoritism over us houndsmen. For instance, gundog is a word that spell check always likes (and it applies to us and the bird hunters). The word houndsmen, which I used just a bit ago, is unknown to the same computer tool. Hey, look at the price of puppies and stud fees for the birddog community and compare those values to our precious beagles, and you will see that the sporting world can, at times, look down their noses at us beaglers. In fact, I have often felt that the hunting beagle is the bastard child of some registries. So, in order to help level the playing field, I have created a small lexicon of terms that are overlooked, and have provided practical definitions of those terms. Perhaps we could add them to *Wikipedia,* or petition publishers of dictionaries to include our beagle specific jargon.

BEAGLER: If you add an "r" to beagle, then the computer goes to red alert, literally, and thinks that you can't spell. A beagler is anyone who is actively engaged in the sport of beagling (see below). A beagler is not the guy next door who keeps a hound on a chain in the yard for nine months and then is flabbergasted that Rover doesn't run rabbits very well during hunting season. A beagler is somewhat psychotic. This is a person who wakes up while dawn has still not yet arrived in Spain, and then drives insane mileage at the chance of winning a ribbon. Or, like me, will haul hounds across several states to hunt, spending hundreds of dollars (not counting fuel for a pickup truck) on a weekend hunt to bring home a few pounds of meat from some species of rabbit or hare not found in his home state. Beaglers have beagle themed knickknacks, salt and pepper shakers, wall art, ties, notepads, coffee mugs, clocks, watches, billfolds, and shirts. In other words, I am talking about those of us who read *The American Beagler*, *Hounds and Hunting*, or other beagle magazines. Please note that the rest of the world thinks we are off center.

BEAGLING: This is the sport practiced by beaglers. It takes on several forms. At the core of the sport is the running of beagles on rabbits. Perhaps you are like me and awake at O'dark-thirty to exercise the hounds before work. Maybe you are more like some friends of mine who run at night because they find it difficult enough to get up in time to make a field trial entry deadline of 8:00 a.m. at a club just down the road (You reading this, Andy Purnell?) There can be great variety in the way we run our beagles. Some of us will follow the beasts as best we can through the briars and thickets to see what our dogs are doing right and where they are at fault. We are the guys who love winter weather because it lets us wear long sleeve shirts to cover the perpetual briar scratches on our arms! I have had people ask me if I have a skin disease in summer due to the brush wounds. Other beaglers like to sit on the tailgate and listen to a good chase. I have to admit that I do this too, especially if there is no threat of a prized hound chasing a rabbit out onto a busy road. I also do this when I have to go do some work that requires dress clothes to work when I am finished running my pack. As a pastor, I have frequently arrived at 9:00 a.m. clergy meetings wearing Dockers, a dress shirt, and wet boots (with tired hounds in the truck's dog box).

Secondary, beagling also involves a great deal of field trialing and hunting. Some of us tend to do one more than the other, but all of us raise beagles for year round enjoyment. I tend to hunt more than trial (I work every Sunday), but I have always found great fun and fellowship at trials when I can attend. Beaglers make habitat for rabbits, take people hunting with hounds as ambassadors for the sport in order to recruit more enthusiasts, and tend to have beagle-related events all over our calendars. In other words, beagling is a lifestyle.

FC: At least in the AKC this is a commonly used title for a Field Champion. Now this ought to imply that the beagle is an awesome rabbit dog. Caution: it may not be the case. If you live in a part of the world that still runs AKC brace trials (traditional brace), then a FC may be a hound unable to find or circle a rabbit. I am not kidding! In Pennsylvania we have a lot of these sorts of beagle clubs still in existence. On occasion, such clubs will tolerate a few gundog beaglers in order to get them to do all the work for their running grounds and trials. A traditional brace beagle is not run frequently for fear that it will get good at it, and a guy with hunting beagles can have the running grounds to himself in these clubs for almost the entire year. A good field champion of the traditional brace sort will stay on a leash until a rabbit is found, be placed on the marked line of a rabbit, and will then bark about 2.2 million times over the distance of 50 feet. At this time (an hour later) the scent will be too cold to continue and the dog will stop and await the leash. If a dog does this slowly enough and often enough to win three trials and amass the 120 points, it will be a field champion!

Alternatively, I have seen field champions that cannot be run outside of a fence because the owner will never see the beast again. These dogs will thunder out of the dog box and run in a straight line until one of two things happens —either it bounces its head off a tree or fence post and must turn, or it jumps a rabbit. Once the rabbit is jumped, it will chase the rabbit very well until the rabbit changes direction. At this point there will be a very long, silent pause in the action. Ten minutes later the chase will resume, and you will not know if the beagle has solved a check or jumped a new rabbit. The better dogs of this sort will be quite good at jumping in front of the dogs that are actually solving checks, and some judges will actually give credit, and wins, to a dog that never solved a check the whole day. Do that process often enough and voila—FC.

Lastly, there are the FC hounds that can run the fur off a rabbit, and these are the hounds we all want to utilize in our breeding programs. All the AKC would have to do is make one extra requirement for a beagle to be a field champion: make all beagles with 3 wins and 120 points jump and solo a rabbit for several circles. They could even make allowances for rabbits going in the hole and other difficulties. There are FCs out there that can't do it!

GUN-SHY: I have seen some awesome dogs that are gun-shy simply because they are owned by non-hunters. I have known people that are not sportsmen who thought that gun-shy was the state of not owning guns, or holding a political stance against gun ownership. As I get older, I find myself a bit gun-shy when it comes to shooting rabbits—every once in a while I just can't kill the little rodents, especially if the freezer is full or the game vest already has a few bunnies weighing it down. In those circumstances, I will often be shy on the trigger and let the rabbit run past, especially if I am afraid that killing more rabbits will result in a shortage of chases the following year. But that is another sort of gun-shy. A dog that bolts for the next county when the gun is fired is definitely gun-shy and not very practical for hunting. I have seen inexperienced judges eliminate a dog from a trial for running towards the gun, but that is the opposite of gun-shy—that is a rabbit wise hound that has put lots of meat on the table!

HUNT 'EM UP: This is a phrase that I yell a lot in the woods to get the dogs excited and keep them working close to me. I often couple this phrase with "hunt with me" or "hunt here" in order to guide the search for rabbits. I suppose the grammar gurus would accept "hunt them up" but who says that? Importantly, the "hunt 'em up" phrase is an antonym of "tally-ho". The distinction is simple: the former says "hey dog, find me a rabbit" while the latter says, "Hey dog I found you a rabbit." I prefer "hunt 'em up". I have known beaglers who own dogs that do not hunt, and they are constantly yelling "Tally-ho!" I have even been to brace and a few gundog brace trials where rabbits are located by sending a skirmish line of stick swinging people into the brush to scare a rabbit from the briars. When the rabbit emerges several people will shout

"TALLY-HO!" as if they just saw the last rabbit on earth. Don't get me wrong, I know the phrase and have taught it to my dogs, but there is no reason to treat the observation of a rabbit with the same awestruck hysterics that would take place if you saw Bigfoot or a unicorn. Hunt 'em up is our phrase of choice.

HOUNDSMAN: This is similar to a beagler, although I suppose it could include owners of other types of hounds too. I prefer to use the term for those of us that take sporting activities with our beagles as our primary sport. I know plenty of beaglers who would rather hunt deer or fish for trout. One can still favor those game species and be a beagler, but those of us who are crazy enough to travel across time zones to hunt swamp rabbits or hare or jackrabbits are houndsmen. We are the guys who hunt deer to eliminate more of them from our rabbit chasing grounds. A houndsman has a life that has quite honestly gone to the dogs.

NBQ: This is fifth place in a trial. It stands for next best qualifier and is worth no points but can get a ribbon. Oftentimes the owner of the NBQ hound is very mad, and can be most upset about the trial results. Only the owner of the second place hound feels more disgust at the abilities of the judges. Trials never cease to amaze me for their ability to create anger and conflict. I have seen born again devout Christians (some of whom feel that Methodists like me are not Christian enough) spin tires for twenty yards as they vacate the trial because they did not win. The annual tonnage of gravel sold to repair this country's beagle club driveways and parking lots may be more that the amount needed to supply the concrete necessary for all construction on our highways. By the end of every trial, there is at least one pothole and maybe even a pair of ruts exiting the clubhouse where someone's truck fishtailed down the lane.

TRIALER: Every time I type this word my computer automatically changes it to trailer. Naturally, this is a person who devotes a great deal of time and energy to field trials. Some of these folks are gravel throwers, but most are just people who share our passion for beagles. I attend few trials (and have had very limited success) but there are beaglers that I see at every single trial I attend. For the most part these are real beaglers doing the hard work of bettering our breed and ensuring that we have great hunting seasons. It helps to be wealthy so that you can miss work and go on the road to be a trialer, but one can also achieve the status by hitting the field trial circuit after retirement or finding a way to earn your living on days that you do not trial. I have also known trialers that can chase hounds all day, climb tree stands to hunt, and carry 100 pounds of dog food at a time that manage to collect disability checks to fund trialing, but that is another story altogether!

Well, I hope that this list of terms will someday be recognized as valid words. I get tired of clicking "ignore" on my spell check. In the meantime, I hope to see you in the field. More than that, I would like to see our hound language make the official lexicons. It seems as if the fly fisherman and birddog enthusiasts are the only sportsmen who get their jargon recognized. But there are more of us. We are the houndsmen beaglers constantly identifying ourselves as trialers in the attempt to avoid gun-shyness in order to produce an FC beagle. Type that previous sentence into your computer and there will be enough red that you will think you are reading the Sermon on the Mount in a red letter Bible!

SUGAR

The beagle nose is legendary. I never cease to be amazed at what a beagle's sense of smell can accomplish. I have seen beagles chase rabbits up cinder roads and watched a pack slow down to a walk in order to continue the pursuit of a rabbit across a coal spoil pile, tonguing on dirt and shale. Years ago, when I was a member at Corning Beagle Club in Corning, NY, we spoke about the graveyard —a rocky section in the large enclosure with very little vegetation. It was a flat but sprawling area and chases often ended there rather quickly. A big nosed beagle could keep the chase moving through that area, and we were always much impressed with the hounds that were able to keep the drive alive through those stones. When you have spoiled house beagles the way I do, there are plenty of other options to see the way that a beagle's acute olfactory system operates.

Cushions are a place where my beagles are constantly getting in trouble. If we come home and find the cushions missing off the couch and chairs, then we know the beagles have struck again. The smallest morsel of food in a cushion will trigger a beagle's appetite and send it into overdrive. They will scatter the cushions across the floor and scavenge into the couch frame for whatever tidbit is left. Very often the scavenged snack is a single kernel of popcorn, or maybe a lone cookie crumb. When we vacuum the furniture it is not as clean as when the beagles give the upholstery a thorough cleaning. We actually have forbidden food in the living room. Not for fear of staining anything, but rather to prevent the dogs from getting a tiny bit of odor that chases them into the cushions like a gopher. Few things are as embarrassing as bringing home a guest to the house only to have them walk through the door and see all the cushions on the floor and the dog sleeping on the couch frame.

The same can be said for the car. Several of my beagles are very car friendly, which is to say that they will sit in the car and not jump on my lap. This is very nice when gas hovers around $4/gallon! I can leave the truck at home and put a dog or two in my wife's car and go to the field. The only problem is that I have a15 year old stepson, and I forgot how much food teenage boys can eat! There have been plenty of mornings when I am driving to the brush in the hour just before dawn only to hear the telltale sound of beagle nails scratching the back seat. I look over my shoulder but it is still dark. The scratching resumes and then pauses. Big snorts ensue, as if the beasts can suck the crumb up from the crack between the seat cushion and the padded back. Or they will lie on their sides and lick under the front bucket seats from the floor behind me, scrounging for whatever scent is under the seat—a single M&M, a lone flake of salt from a previously consumed French fry, or maybe the cap from a drained bottle of flavored water or soda pop. Always there is the scratch-scratch, snort, sniff, scratch-scratch, snort, and sniff. And then the long tongue reaching like a hand to find the source of the odor.

To be honest, I think beagles are especially fond of nasty smells. Anything rotting in the field is a choice place to roll around. The same holds true for the worst smelling scat. Garbage cans are an endless source of delight, and I am constantly hiding my boots from dogs who love to stuff their heads into the footwear and snort away.

Beagles are stomachs with the necessary locomotion and food sensing gear needed to fill said stomach. Vacations are a difficult thing to manage when you have beagles, and we once hired a kennel that utilized one of those automatic food dispensers. When we returned a week later our hounds looked like stuffed sausages.

"What happened to my dogs?" I asked looking at the massive beagle bellies.

"I didn't notice until day two." The kennel owner said in disbelief, making hand gestures of a circle growing in diameter.

"What? You didn't notice what?" I implored.

"They never stopped eating. The directions say that dogs eat less with these feeders. Your dogs just sat on their hind ends and kept eating!" He gave body language trying to show how beagles sit on their backsides, and he opened and closed his mouth loudly as he described their refusal to quit eating. I could have predicted this had I known he used those feeders, which is why I told the man how much food to feed each dog when I left. I had also told him that they will beg and look sad and starving even if they had enough food already. I loaded the obese hounds into the truck and headed for home. As I left the owner of the kennel just waved at me saying, "Honest, they just kept eating, I couldn't believe it."

Those of us who own beagles do believe it. I have used hot dogs to train my dogs any number of commands, and I learned long ago that the way to a beagle's obedience is through his gut! But there have been other ways that beagles have impressed me with their keen sense of smell. On two separate incidents my dog Rebel has awoken me by scratching my cheek. On both occasions I was almost immediately diagnosed with a sinus infection. It was the only two times he ever did that. Sure enough, years later, his puppy did the same thing. I think they could smell the infection, and no one will convince me otherwise.

Just today my oldest beagle had a couple of rotten teeth extracted. When he came home and was reintroduced to the pack they all commenced to smelling him. No, not in the places where dogs typically smell one another, they all sniffed vigorously along his cheeks. They could smell the stitches in his gums that the vet had put in after the surgery. I suppose this is why beagles are used in airports to find food, and why they have been trained to find termites in houses. It is a legendary olfactory system. But here is my favorite anecdote that demonstrates the strength of the beagle nose: one of my church members, Doug Williams, is a Marine. He spent a year in Iraq (a bit over a year, actually). When he was getting ready to return to the United States he mailed a bunch of things home. Some of the boxes arrived and his beagle, Sugar, paid very little attention to those boxes. Then a box arrived that drove her nose crazy. She jumped repeatedly until the box fell to the floor and then she did the dance that we have all seen from beagles as they circle the source of the odor and wag their tails in that circular, agitated fashion that shows excitement.

Her owner had left well over a year ago—there were months of active duty stateside before deployment in Iraq. When Doug's parents opened the box they found a pair of his boots inside. Those boots were saturated with the scent of their son and Sugar knew it. Doug is home. I look forward to the Fourth of July every year, mostly for the thrill of fireworks and the chance to eat barbeque. I pray every night that these wonderful young men and women all come home soon to their loved ones. Sugar taught me that boots are not valued for their stink; they are prized because they have a connection to the person who wears them. May all the boots come home, and with the soldiers who wear them still alive. Thanks to all the veterans for all that you do. Please come home soon.

TANNING HIDES

Those of us who routinely hunt are part of a fading culture. Sure, you can watch people hunting on television, whispering to avoid the detection of a massive buck as it follows the trail of hay that is dumped daily along a path past the Taj Mahal deer stands that litter the private hunting club. I often wonder how many commercials those guys have to sell to pay for a single hunting trip. Us regular folk hunt near home on land that we can access, and I hope that this will continue long into the future, but I fear hunting may become a wealthy man's game. But, that is another story.

At any rate, those of us who hunt and live even partially off the land are a dying breed. There are a few skills that I think most of us have—the ability to catch fish, take a deer, identify some wild mushrooms that are edible, preserve wild berries, call in a turkey, and hunt rabbits with great success. This is far more food-gathering than most city and suburban dwellers do in a year. I live close to State College, home of Penn State University, and I often refrain from talks about hunting when in that town. I can't tell you how many people have voiced their opinion that hunting is unethical as they shove a half-pound of burger into their mouth.

"At least wild animals know they are food," I might offer.

"So, *you* killed them!" was the rebuttal, muffled by a mouthful of food.

"Your burger didn't die of old age in a pasture and grind itself—somebody killed the cow," I counter, but to no avail. I try to spend my time with like-minded spirits who enjoy the outdoors and hunting as much as I do. Last fall I managed to find some private property to hunt, a place that is owned by Gruff. While there, I learned that some people know a lot more about the wild. I am not sure what

Gruff's real first name is. He is a retired logger, and his homestead is a rabbit hunting paradise. Gruff lives almost entirely off the land, and rarely goes to town. If you see him in town, it is probably at the beer distributor, discount cigarette store, bakery, and yard sales or at church. Gruff was in church one Sunday and he informed me, while shaking hands at the back of the church after worship, that I could come hunt rabbits at his place anytime I wanted. I didn't go—I had no idea where he lived and he wasn't in church very often. Sometime later, Lenny and I were lamenting the lack of shooting in the early season. The weeds were thick and the hounds were having great chases but the vegetation was too abundant to provide much shooting. The dogs would thunder past me, a mere ten yards away. Who knows how far ahead the rabbit was —I never heard or saw it.

"We need some new spots to try until the snow knocks down this cover," Lenny said as he lifted his hounds into their wire pens after we drove to his place.

"Yeah, but you know me," I said, "I am scared to run close to the hardtop roads."

"Another farm would be nice," Lenny lifted another beagle into the pen for the night. I nodded my head in agreement.

"Know that Gruff who drives the old pickup with the lumber bed that he built after the metal one rusted?" I asked

"Yeah, old man Mackenzie," Lenny said as he filled water bowls.

"Where does he live?" I asked as I filled another water bowl.

"Way out past the clay road on some spot he timbered just before he retired," Lenny said.

"He have rabbits? Cuz he told me I could hunt rabbits there anytime"

Lenny looked at me with bugged eyes, "Old Man Mackenzie gave you permission to hunt?"

"Yeah, in church."

Now his eyes really bugged and spun around as he spit the words, "You saw Gruff in *church*!?"

"Sure, he comes more than you do, probably at least four times each year. He just offered me hunting permission a few weeks ago. I would like to visit him."

"And you will," Lenny said, "tomorrow morning at 8 a.m. I will pick you up at 7:00. Bring your good dogs—wait, you don't have any good dogs. HAHAHA."

"Should we call him first, invite him to hunt too?" I asked.

"Call him? He has no phone. I ain't even sure he has running water or postal service," Lenny said, "But he has rabbits!"

When we got to Gruff's house my ball cap was squashed from bouncing off the ceiling of the truck. To call the path we took to Gruff's small cabin a road would be too kind. It was a series of flat stones that were sometimes level. I staggered out of Lenny's truck, perhaps suffering from a concussion. Gruff met us at the porch; no doubt he heard our arrival as Lenny dropped the big diesel into low gear to get up the last rise.

"Oh good," Gruff said as he patted me on the back, "You guys came in the front way, the back road is a little rough from the rain," he pointed towards what looked like a two foot deep deer trail snaking into the woods.

We went inside for coffee that was boiling on a wood cooking-stove. Gruff had a hand pump for water a la *Little House on the Prairie*. There was no electricity, and kerosene lamps were sitting on various counters and ledges. Only one of them was lit, as light poured through the eastern window. I was nervous from the cliffs and drop-offs that we just traversed, and the coffee only amplified the feeling. He could tell it was too strong for me and kindly opened a can of condensed milk. I poured it into the cup. The color of the coffee never changed, and it stirred like molasses because it was so thick.

"Don't you go feeling bad for me Preacher," Gruff said as I looked around, "I love it here. I choose not to have power. I don't need mail if I don't have utilities!" His pantry was massive and contained dried pasta, rice, flour, sugar— the sort of thing that would not spoil without a refrigerator. Also, there were more canning jars full of vegetables than I had ever seen before (or since).

41

"Wow. That's a lot of jars." My jaw dropped.

"Yard sales," he said, "Dirt cheap at yard sales. Those vegetables are the reason you should have no trouble shooting rabbits. C'mon."

Gruff led us around back to a massive, sprawling garden. There were still a few tomatoes hanging into the fall, but there were also salad greens, winter squash and pumpkins. Much of the garden was finished for the season, but remnants of pepper plants, squash vines, beans and other vegetables could be seen stacked into a compost pile. I spied a few peas that he must have planted late. A fat rabbit ran into the briars. Upon closer examination, I noticed that the briars were blackberries, and beyond the blackberries were blueberry bushes, and then I saw an apple orchard, and it just went out from there. Cover was everywhere, and lots of shooting lanes could be found too. "Gruff you want to hunt with us?" I asked

"Sure, I will be back." He walked into the small house and emerged with a pump shotgun. We let the dogs out of the truck and entered the blackberries. Soon six dogs were chasing in full cry and split onto two different rabbits. I waited by a brace of beagles—one of Lenny's dogs and one of mine. Lenny waited with the pack of four. Gruff stood by the "back road" to his house. By noon we had 12 rabbits, each of us taking a limit. The chases were great, the cover incredible. That little farm had more varieties of fruit trees and berry bushes than I can remember. We watered the dogs and Gruff invited us in for lunch.

He boiled egg noodles and poured canned venison and canned mushrooms over the top. It was delicious. That kitchen cooking-stove was hot enough to over-heat the whole house on a mild autumn day, so we ate on the porch. Dishes went into the kitchen sink and water was boiled to clean them.

Gruff emerged with a little knife, "Waters boiling, I put more coffee on too. Let's clean these rabbits." I shivered at the thought of a second cup of coffee.

We sat down to clean them and Gruff just about fell off the porch when I ripped the hide off a cottontail.

"What's wrong?" I gasped nervously. He was clearly disturbed and still holding that knife.

"Don't you tan the hides?"

His words cut through me to a childhood memory I had erased. As a kid, I had vocational plans of living like Jeremiah Johnson. As previously mentioned, I wanted to be a mountain man. At one point, I had been given a leather deer hide, and my intent was to cut it into a hat and gloves, and then line both sides with rabbit fur. We had two beagles and I tried to save every hide from every rabbit. I had some salt and alum to pickle the hides, although dad thought I was crazy for the idea. He merely said, "Keep that damn science experiment in the farting tool shed and not in the house." Only he didn't say farting.

The only thing that had more holes than my rabbit hides were my fingers. Rabbit hide tears easily so I was trying to slice fur while prying with my fingers. Each venture ended with more human blood on the hides than rabbit. I considered making the hat and gloves from squirrels, but they have the opposite problem—too tight and not very warm in comparison to rabbit. I soaked my hides in the brine each night. But let's be honest, they weren't entire hides—more like chunks of fur by the time I mangled them in the skinning process.

Fleshing them made the hides even smaller and more perforated. I could see roots from the hair in various places. Even so I kept at it. Eventually I had quite a storehouse of tanned rabbit hides. I brought them in the house all in a bundle across my hands. My intent was to look like a fur trader from the Rocky Mountains emerging into rendezvous with my cache of pelts for trade. My mother was in the kitchen making supper, she ran into the living room screaming, "Get that dead animal out of my house!" Apparently she had no education in her middle school years about mountain man rendezvous. I couldn't really see her retreat, because my glasses had fogged up in the house after bringing the hides into the warm kitchen through the cold winter air. It sounded like a few things fell.

"Mom, It's fine. It is time to make my hat and gloves."

She poked her head around the corner. "What did your father tell you about that project?"

"He said to keep it outside." Just then, Dad arrived home from work.

"Whaddya think I was kidding? OUTSIDE with that stuff!" He growled. Only he didn't say stuff.

"But the science project is over," I pleaded. "The hides are tanned. All we gotta do now is have mom sew them onto the buckskin to make the hat and gloves."

I could tell by the way mom stuttered that she wasn't touching those hides, "N-n-o w-w-w-way. My s-s-s-s-sewing machine is g-g-going near that."

"Out," Dad said calmly.

"But Dad, the hides are tanned," I pleaded.

"I'm gonna show you a tanned hide..."

I left to the shed. The hides really were tanned quite well, even if they were not all intact. I commenced to making the hat and gloves by hand in the basement. Dad at least let me bring the hides in the basement when he saw that they really were preserved. The finished gloves were never functional. The fur looked great on the outside, but I couldn't line the inside very well. In addition, one glove looked more like a mitten, and there contained too much space in some finger slots and not enough in others. That detail was hard to notice though, because the outside of the gloves was overflowing with rabbit fur.

The hat was another story. I was low on rabbit fur, but the inside was lined quite well and was very warm. The outside was a bit bald in places. Imagine, if you will, the hat that Goober wore on *The Andy Griffith Show*, but with grey cotton balls placed haphazardly on the outside. It looked sort of like that. As I said, my hides were somewhat fragmented in the skinning process. My folks hated it, but I wore them. I shoveled snow with the hat and gloves, and although the gloves were not much good for anything but stopping the wind, my head was very warm. I even had earflaps that were long enough to cover most of my face, even though the right one was noticeably longer than the left.

One time I came in and heard my sister talking on the phone to a neighbor, "No, he gets real good grades in school, and we think he is normal sometimes. No, mom never dropped him. Nope, he takes regular classes. The hat is homemade, how could you tell? You too, have a good day." Memories...

"HEY!" Gruff was snapping his fingers in my face, "You taking a fit or something?"

"What?" I asked.

"Weren't you paying attention?" Gruff quizzed me, "Lenny and I cleaned all these things while you stared off into space. I said the hides are real soft. Do you want any?"

"Umm, no you can have them. I think my wife feels the same way about rabbit hides as my mother did," I winced at her potential reaction to hides.

"Lenny don't want 'em either, I'll take them all then." Gruff had the rabbit meat packed into bags for transport.

"Can you make hats and gloves out of the rabbit hides?" I asked Gruff.

"Sure," he said.

"I will pay you for them if you can," I replied, "I can't wait to go to my sister's house and clean her sidewalks and driveway next winter."

45

TRICK-OR-TREAT

Halloween is hurtling towards us, tearing through the calendar at a rapid pace. I know that many pastors are outraged at Halloween, feeling that it is a day devoted to the devil. I have never harbored such beliefs, feeling that the main thrust of the holiday involves children consuming way too much sugar while dressed as their favorite superhero or some other character. Mostly, for me, Halloween marks the calendar as a spot near the beginning of the long awaited rabbit season. The opening day of rabbit has migrated slightly in Pennsylvania, but has traditionally hovered near the last Saturday in October, or the first Saturday in November. Therefore, in the midst of all the Halloween hurry, I am busy trying to prepare a perfect first day of the hunting season.

The first big problem about Halloween is the omnipresent bags of trick-or-treat candy. Chocolate, of course, is toxic to dogs. My faithful hunting hounds live in the house, and have displayed remarkable skill at locating and devouring any and all food (this includes dog food, human food, and garbage). Halloween is one of the biannual gluts of candy. The other great candy gathering season is Easter, and when the sum total of these two holidays is combined, the end result is the never ending supply of stale and outdated candy stashed into drawers and cabinets.

In our house the candy must be stowed in the cabinet above the refrigerator. This is for two reasons. First, this is the safest of all possible places to keep chocolate away from the beagles. The same stubborn tenacity that allows my pack to chase a rabbit until it is either dead or in a hole will also enable them to access food from almost any normal storage area. The uppermost cabinet is safe.

Secondly, this is the only spot that somewhat prevents my family from devouring the candies before the big night of crime when costumed hooligans mug homeowners on their own porches. At some point this cache of sugar will be discovered by either my wife or stepson; I can tell when this happens because I hear the kitchen chair sliding across the linoleum floor to serve as a makeshift ladder against the refrigerator door for the purpose of looting the trick-or-treat supplies; although my stepson has now surpassed the height of his mother and can open the canine-proof cabinet without the aid of a stepladder.

This pilfering of the candies amounts to extra anxiety as the miniature chocolate bars are left on tables and counters where beagles are quite capable of locating and consuming them wrappers and all. For those of you who have never had the opportunity to call a veterinarian with the fear of a potential lethal dose of chocolate coursing through the veins of your prized rabbit dog, I can tell you that the advice I received was to use a turkey-baster to force hydrogen peroxide into the dog's stomach until it induces sufficient vomiting that even the wrapper (or multiple wrappers) are expelled from the mutt and onto your kitchen linoleum. Beagles love vomit, and find regurgitated chocolate to be even tastier than the first time it was served. It must be similar to the way that I prefer reheated chili to fresh chili—it gets better with time.

One remedy for mitigating the incidents of chocolate consumption by the beagles is to keep them tired—*dog tired*. October is a great time of year to build endurance in the hounds after the long summer of very short chases. It is also a favorite month to locate the perfect spot for the opening day of rabbit season. A summer spent inside the beagle club is very convenient for jumping rabbits quickly, before the morning sun makes the temperature soar, but it does nothing for scouting wild rabbits to pursue on the opening day. October is a month that finds me exploring new brush piles, as I investigate the places where I found rabbit tracks in the late February snow last winter. I figure any place that still had lots of rabbits at the end of the cold season will have plenty in the early fall!

Pranks, of course, are a vital part of Halloween for me. I like things more complex than juvenile acts of covering a yard in toilet paper. I had a great one last year. A friend of mine, Bubba Armstrong, is a serious deer hunter. He hunts all the seasons—archery, rifle, and muzzleloader. One problem for me is the fact that many of his Archery deer stands are in places where I rabbit hunt, and since the seasons overlap, this can be a problem. A year ago my wife returned home with a bag of dog treats that cost a small fortune from one of the massive pet stores. Rawhides, pig ears, soft chewy morsels, and cow hooves. Yes, cow hooves, or halves of cow hooves, filled with rock hard peanut butter. I watched the beagles gnaw on these delicacies for hours, and was amazed that such a thing could exist. Archery season was rapidly approaching, and I was anxious about keeping Bubba in the big timber and away from my prized briars. Then I was struck with inspiration.

Bubba is obsessed with hunting shows on television. He has been thoroughly drenched in the culture that identifies deer by a number. I might say, "Oh, there goes an eight point buck!" Bubba would say something like "That's about a 130 score." I don't understand the system he uses, but it is quite the dominant topic on the programs he watches. He is also always talking about "symmetry" and all sorts of names for the tines on the antlers of a deer. I decided to give Bubba evidence of a buck with a score of a million and six.

I took two cow hoof halves so that I could make tracks of one entire cow hoof. I waited for a rain to pass and then hiked out to one of Bubba's archery stands—the one furthest from my early season honey holes for rabbits. I used a small scrap of plywood to cover the mud and support my weight so that I could make fake cow tracks without leaving footprints—*voila*, evidence of a massive buck! That was not enough, following the logic that big bucks make rubs on big trees, I proceeded to take a pair of brush cutters and create buck rubs on trees that no normal whitetail could possible spar against. Eight and ten inch diameter birch trees were made to look as if they had been thrashed by the king of the forest. I even rubbed a tree over a foot in diameter near the tree that held his actual stand.

Bubba was real quiet for the first few weeks of archery, he never said a word, but I did notice that he was consistently at the tree stand that I altered. I figured this out by walking a ridge slightly above his tree stand. I was well over a hundred yards away and hidden by a thick clump of evergreens. Using binoculars I looked through the pines to see him in the stand. I swallowed a laugh as I fell down a leafy slope, and then bowling balled through a stand of dead saplings that were victims of the porcupines. The fall came to a rest in some greenbrier and I made a "WHOOSH" sound from pain.

I saw my hunting buddy the next day at the local restaurant "Hey Bubba, haven't seen you out at the old coal strippings where I hunt rabbits." I said.

"Come here!" Bubba thought he was whispering as he summoned me with a wild hand wave towards himself. His hearing is not keen from years of loud working environments, so his whispers are quite loud, "I'm on to a massive buck. World class!"

"Good for you Bubba!" I encouraged, "Did you see him yet."

"Nah, but I heard him yesterday. Sounded like a train in the woods," Bubba said, "He musta been hot on some does, and when he stopped running he made the loudest buck snort I ever heard!" Obviously I had fallen louder than I thought if Bubba heard me. On the last day of archery Bubba killed a twelve point that was bigger than any deer I ever saw in the woods. He found it a disappointment. I stopped by his place when he butchered the beast; it was so big that its front shoulders were entirely on the ground when hung from the pavilion Bubba uses to process deer.

"Wow!" I said, "What a monster."

Bubba held the deer's hoof in his hands and shook his head in disgust, "He's so-so."

Bubba spent the whole winter and summer dreaming of the humungous buck that got away.

My big prank this Halloween season will be to sneak a nice side-by-side .410 into the house. I bought it used, but it is in perfect condition. I have always been a solid fan of 16 gauge shotguns, but the extremely light .410 seems ideal to carry in the early season when the cover is so thick that I can't shoot beyond twenty yards. My only concern is that it is a purchase not approved by the Marital Board of Finance. The board consists of one member: my wife. If the board were to discover this infraction, then I would be assigned a date in Marital Court. The Marital Court has one judge, one prosecuting attorney, and one jury member. My wife holds all three positions. I have never been a plaintiff in Marital Court, only the defendant. I am hoping to introduce the new gun soon, and let it acclimate to the other guns. I will leave it in a soft carrying case near the gun safe, the way you might allow a new fish to remain in a bag while it soaked in your aquarium at home to prevent sudden shock upon release.

It is also my hope that Renee sees the gun case (which I have owned for years) so often that she presumes the gun inside is also a long-term resident. On the day before rabbit season I might ask her, "Where in the world is my shotgun case? I gotta hunt tomorrow." Then, if the plan hatches correctly, she will grab the case and say, "You'd lose your head if it weren't attached."

Hey, the vows say "in sickness and in health" and I clearly have a sickness for nice double barrel shotguns. I just hope I can shoot well with the little gun. Don't praise me just yet; odds are good that I will get busted in this scam. My trick may not yield a treat. She is not as easy to fool as Bubba, which reminds me, I have to buy some cow hoof treats.

TURKEY DAY

When I was a child we would routinely mix a few table scraps into the dog's food. Trimmed meat fat, bacon grease, gristle, gravy, and fish skin were fairly routine additions to the dry kibbles. In those days there were still butchers, and chicken wings were cheap—no one had heard that Buffalo had discovered a way to make it the most expensive part of a chicken. They were often free if you bought some thighs or breasts. Chicken hearts and livers were even cheaper. Winter months meant frozen water bowls in the kennel during the overnight hours, and we often served the beagles a supper of dry dog food floating in a broth of chicken organs. The water bowls were changed at supper and the broth helped the dogs stay hydrated since the drinking water would be frozen by morning. I had to dump the ice and replace it with fresh water every morning before school. I remember thumping the bowls against each other as the ice landed at my feet, looking like a misshapen, massive hockey puck.

My current beagles live in the house and they still get lots of table scraps mixed in with their supper. Lenny was at my house for an early spring cookout. It was probably a bit too cold to cook outside, but cabin fever had convinced us to get out and give it a whirl. There was also the extra bonus that the air was too chilly for our wives to accompany us to the yard, and so they remained inside. Lenny brought a cooler of his favorite beverage, which he secretly retrieved from the trunk of his wife's car after she was out of sight. The beverage must have made him even colder but he acted as if it warmed him. I flipped the steaks and watched my breath steam into the air, and then sipped my coffee. Just then Lenny noticed that I had trimmed the cooked steaks and placed the gristle in a pile.

"Want me to throw that out for you?" He said, "I'm going in the house to refill this coffee mug so my wife thinks I am drinking the stuff." He dumped his cup of coffee on the lawn, which was not yet green from the winter cold.

"Sure, but get me a coffee and put the gristle in the fridge, would ya?" I asked as I handed him the bowl full of scraps and my empty mug, "The pups can have it tonight."

"Are you nuts?" He yelled, "That's venison! Aren't you worried about turning your dogs into deer runners?"

"Nah," I said, "That's just an old wives' tale. Eating venison won't make a dog run deer."

"Yeah it will," Lenny said, "Once they get a taste for it."

"How's come my dogs never chase a cow? They've eaten lots of beef."

Lenny stared at me blankly; I could see the wheels churning in his mind. He scratched his head and said, "Cuz cows don't run from beagles, or else they would be running cows."

"Ever seen a beagle run a pig on any farm you been to?" I asked.

"I've seen beagles chase chickens and kill them," Lenny countered and folded his arms smugly.

"We bought that dog food on sale with the lamb meat in it," I retorted, "We've never had our dogs chase sheep even when we hunt on farms that raise them."

"You better not feed 'em anything you don't want 'em chasing," he cautioned.

"I fed my mutts some fat from a bear roast that I was given, and the last time a bear was in my yard they barked and retreated at the same time."

"Figures," Lenny said, "Your dogs would be cowards."

And with that last bit of reasoning we agreed to disagree. I felt that the meat was not an enticement to the chase, and Lenny felt it was. I was more convinced that scent pads were the main concern; Lenny felt the whole animal was a risk. I never gave it another thought.

A little later into the spring Lenny and I decided to anger the beagles and become turkey hunters. This is always problematic for me, because my beagles are convinced that they own my truck, and that they have exclusive rights to that vehicle for the several hours that precede and follow the rising of the sun. When I lace up my boots and grab a shotgun the dogs all erupt in a chorus of excitement. The chorus turns into a dirge as I sneak outside without them and they hear the engine start without them in the dog box.

I realize that married couples have many disagreements about such serious topics as parenting, marriage, and finances; but my marriage with Renee is most seriously tested when I leave at o' dark-thirty in the morning to go turkey or deer hunting, or trout fishing. She is left alone with a pack of beagles that commence to running the perimeter of every room in the house at full cry as they attempt to find a way outside in order to find me. It was one evening in deer season when Renee and I had the following conversation:

"Why don't you go out tonight," she said, "Stay out with the guys as late as you want."

"I don't want to go out tonight," I respond, "I hafta get up early to hunt."

"No, please go out. Go to a bar, or some place of low morals."

"Honey, I would never do that," I said, "I can't stay up late, I get tired."

"Try," she replied, "I will make you some coffee. Go find a deer camp and play cards."

"I hate deer camps, you know that," I sputtered. "Those guys snore all night and stink of smoke and bacon so bad they never see deer."

"I would rather you stay out late and pursue the sins of the flesh than leave early in the morning!" she spat at me. Her eyes were puffy and bloodshot.

"Are you feeling sick?" I voiced concern.

"I haven't slept past 4.a.m since deer season started!"

Apparently the dogs jump on her when I leave in an effort to enlist her help so that she can inform me that I forgot them at the house when I left. This is an ongoing marital difficulty that has not found a resolution. She is looking into the possibility of finding me a private hunting camp just for me. There was mention of me taking the dogs there too. I told her we can't afford a hunting camp, and she suggested a garden shed would be sufficient. Her plan is to purchase a quarter acre and put a little wooden shed on the property with a cheap wire fence around the perimeter for the beagles. I will be exiled to this property any time I plan on leaving early in the morning without the beagles. In my youth I was very selective about what deer I shot, but now I fill my tags as quickly as possible—she has threatened to change the locks to the house while I am hunting if she becomes too sleep deprived.

"Sweetheart, I want a nice buck," I whined at the threat.

"If it's brown, it's down!" She countered, "Kill a deer and end the season."

It was with that conversation in my memory that I shot a little Jake turkey during spring gobbler season. Lenny held out, and was able to kill a massive gobbler with a beard that drug on the ground. There wasn't much meat on my bird so I served it a la high school cafeteria. I am not sure about your school, but mine had all of one holiday meal—turkey gravy over mashed potatoes. This was done in an attempt to stretch the meat further. That is pretty sad, when you consider that grocery stores give turkeys away. What meat could be cheaper? The upside of turkey gravy was that it was never dry.

Which brings me back to Lenny's big gobbler. He cut the big bird into pieces the way that a chicken might be processed. The end result was two thighs, two drumsticks, and two pieces of breast meat. He decided to cook the bird on his gas grill. He called me down to try out the delicacy. He had already eaten when I arrived. Most of the gobbler appeared to be uneaten. I took a bite.

"Whaddya think?" Lenny said.

The thought that came to my mind was, "They should use this stuff to clean up toxic spills. It is a damn super sponge that has robbed my mouth of all saliva." I chewed and chewed, however, and thought about my response, "It's real good." I fibbed. I cut the next piece into the size of an aspirin. I swallowed it with a gulp of Pepsi. I then cut the next piece a little smaller and repeated the process until I finished the thigh that I was given. The drumsticks were harder than actual musical drumsticks.

"You really like it?" Lenny said.

"Oh yeah," I said in my most polite pastoral voice, "It's delicious."

"Good, you can take the rest home," he said, "My wife doesn't like wild turkey—birds or liquor!"

When I did return to my house, I cut the leg meat off the bone. This process only required me to sharpen my knife three times. The blade dragged through the meat and actually cut into the bone easier than the flesh. I put all the meat in the refrigerator, which only dried it out even further. After refrigerating the bird, I sat in the living room with my wife. I belched about four times.

"Good Lord, you have a lot of gas," she said.

"Sorry, I had a two liter of Pepsi at Lenny's house." She looked at me as if I was a glutton. She had no idea what I had been through.

I thought hard about throwing the meat away, and then I was struck with inspiration—dog treats!

I will be the first to admit that my hunting dogs are spoiled. They get pig ears, rawhides, and cow hooves to gnaw upon in the evening. None of those items, which cost good money from a pet store, lasted as long as the breast meat from Lenny's turkey. Don't tell my wife, but it took my prized Rebel three nights to eat the one half-breast. I simply put the remaining meat in a Ziploc bag labeled, "Dog Treat" and buried it in the vegetable crisper. I worried each night that she might find the partially chewed meat in the refrigerator.

The mere thought of her finding the turkey breast gave me flashbacks of the great fishing bait debacle that occurred not long after we got married. They say that the mind protects us from painful memories by inducing amnesia so that we do not recall traumatic events. All I can remember with certainty about the fishing bait debacle was that the take-home container that held the coleslaw from the church chicken barbeque looked identical to the container of wax worms that I had placed in the refrigerator door. I also seem to remember her wanting to pour her coleslaw on top of her chicken. I have vague memories of screaming and the sensation of pain on my head. At any rate, the turkey breast in the crisper drawer had me walking on eggshells until Rebel finished eating it. Looking back, I should have just put the thing on top of the refrigerator each night—beef jerky has more moisture than Lenny's turkey did, it never would have spoiled.

We were rapidly approaching the fall turkey season and something remarkable happened. Rebel has always been the kind of dog that would trail grouse, pheasant, and woodcock; but he seems to have taken a special liking to birds since spring. There have been a dozen mornings this summer when Rebel has chased turkey across the cornfields. This has caused me to rethink Lenny's premise that feeding certain meat to a dog will make it chase that animal.

Granted, there is a lot of turkey in the woods this year. I have had longer delays in my morning commutes to work due to turkey crossings than I have for school buses. The buses stop and one or two kids get on board and off the yellow behemoth goes to the next house. It seems that there are no central bus stops anymore where a score of kids gather, rather the bus stops at each child's individual home, whereupon the bus driver does everything short of running up to the front door and escorting the student to the bus. Turkey delays, however, occur when a dozen hens cross the road, each leading a dozen little poults. That adds up to a gross of turkey walking single file across the road. This might happen several times before reaching a main highway.

When it does happen, I always stop the vehicle in awe, because when I was a child there were very few turkeys in Pennsylvania. In fact, seeing a turkey track was something to brag about. So, it could be that Lenny was right, or it could be that there are just so many turkeys that Rebel's love of upland birds was bound to expand. I blame it on the bird feeder we fill for the songbirds each winter. He loves to smell the ground around the bird feeder in the yard. He has been this way since he was a puppy.

Lenny and I were running dogs the other day when Rebel thundered through the valley on a sight chase just behind a big gobbler. The bird ponderously lifted off the ground and flew over the tree line. The only thing more awkward looking than a turkey taking off is a goose landing. Geese land as if they have never done it before, and with the trepidation that anything might happen as they scoot across the surface of the water. Their loud honks seem to be saying, "LOOK OUT BELOW, I'VE NEVER LANDED BEFORE!"

"Say Lenny," I sighed, "Do you think a .22 Hornet would tear up a rabbit too bad?"

"I'd say so, why?" He asked.

"Well, we can use rifles to hunt turkey in the fall, and it is the same time of year as rabbit season. I am considering taking Reb out for turkey. He will probably chase more rabbits than birds though, and I want to be ready. I don't have an over/under turkey gun that combines a rifle with a shotgun."

"Just take a 12 gauge, we will probably see turkey close enough to get one," Lenny said.

"Yeah, but you are only allowed to shoot one turkey in the fall, I figured I would take a long range rifle and just fill that tag first before concentrating on rabbits," I reasoned.

"A .22 Hornet? That is a pretty big gun for rabbits. I have seen guys use a .22 and head-shoot rabbits sitting in front of the dogs, but a Hornet is big enough to kill a deer!"

"Yeah, I know," I scratched my chin, "My cousin Cindy used to hunt deer with one. She ain't very big, and the .22 Hornet doesn't kick very much. She would head or neck-shoot her deer."

"I got a better idea," Lenny said, "Why don't we just go for turkey one day and get both our tags filled. The woods are full of 'em. Hey, we could deep fry them for Thanksgiving!"

"They are supposed to stay moist that way," I said, remembering his spring gobbler prepared as jerky, "But you gotta be careful about starting a grease fire."

"If you're worried about a fire I will mix up some more barbeque sauce and cook them on the grill like that spring gobbler, you really like it that way," Lenny said, obviously pleased to have been a good host. I shuddered at the thought of drinking another two liters of soda pop in one sitting.

"Nah, we can manage the deep fryer!" I beamed.

"Great, we will skip rabbits on the first day of turkey season and just hunt turkey," Lenny said, "We'll leave the dogs at home and head for the timber where I keep seeing a big flock."

"I can't do that."

"Do what?" He asked.

"Hunt turkey without the dogs," I said.

"Why not?" He looked confused.

"Cuz my wife has been getting estimates on those pre-fabricated wooden garden sheds that the Amish make."

WHISKERS' HOWL

It was during the Fourth of July holiday that I first became acquainted with a beagle, the first hound that I ever saw run a rabbit. Now, I must begin this story with a bit of a disclaimer, a qualifying statement if you will: I grew up in western Pennsylvania. This is significant because there was a time period in the late seventies and into the eighties when many folks in western PA felt that a AKC registered beagle was synonymous with "can't run a rabbit." I am, of course, referring to the waning days of brace trials. Those AKC trials sent many serious hunters away from registered hounds and into the world of "un-papered" beagles. I sympathize with their decisions, but wish that more people would have been aware of true hunting, AKC registered hounds that did thrive in other parts of the country at that time.

Anyway, one of my neighbors, John Dubler, had an AKC registered hound named Whiskers. Whiskers lived, by and large, on a rope in the small front yard. This is where John and his wife would spend much of their time, and Whiskers was there too, on a laundry line that gave him ample room to roam the entire yard and porch. At night, Whiskers was taken to the miniscule back yard that had just enough room to hold a 4' x 8' above ground, wire-floored kennel for Whiskers to sleep in. Every morning and every evening (except during the coldest and wettest weather) Whiskers got to go for a walk. If you said the word "walk" the old beagle would let out a deep, short woof, signaling his eagerness to walk.

This caused difficulty, because if John would say, "I am going to clean up in the kitchen and then go for a walk," Whiskers would proceed to bark until John finished his work. So the Dubler's began to spell the word "W-A-L-K" like you would around a child from whom you might try to hide a bad word. This was to no avail either, as Whisker's learned to spell "W-A-L-K" too. When out on a walk, John

would let Whiskers off his leash to chase rabbits while
John himself would meander back and forth to watch the
chase. At certain times of the year, John would pick
strawberries, June berries, Teaberries, blueberries or
raspberries while Whiskers chased his rabbit. The Dublers
had the best Jelly in town, and a tired beagle.

Sometimes, John would have to leave Whiskers on the
chase at dark and go home. Somehow, Whiskers always
made it to the porch by morning and would scratch at the
door. But he always avoided the cars. I went with John and
watched Whiskers. Now, by western Pennsylvania
standards of the time (and maybe the present) Whiskers
had lightning speed, which is to say that you actually had
to jog to keep up with Whiskers.

"I got this pokey little dog for free," John told me as we
watched Whiskers trot down a grassy path tonguing the
line.

"How come he was free?" I asked, eyes wide open,
hoping to find a place full of free beagles.

"Well, the breeder started Whiskers and decided he was
way too fast for trials," John answered.

"Hmm. Well, he doesn't seem too fast, we keep track of
him quite easy. He was even kinda slow there for quite a
stretch," I offered, not knowing enough about beagles to
even be aware of the fact that I had insulted the man's
hound. Even so, I would have my first beagle not too long
after that day.

"Yeah, well I am kinda slow anymore too," John said.
"Whiskers is enough for me. Besides, he doesn't lose any
rabbits." John must have been in his late seventies at the
time, and he would be painting his two-story house on a
ladder years later—his slowing down was pretty active.
Perhaps no one could keep up with him when he was 18.

All of that being said, it is also true that the first time I
became aware of Whiskers was when he started howling on
John's porch on the Fourth of July. I believe that fireworks
are illegal in Pennsylvania, but that doesn't stop anyone
from using them. My neighborhood echoed with little
explosions all day long as people detonated firecrackers
and M-80's, cherry bombs, and every other imaginable
contraption with a fuse. We kids got smoke bombs and

snakes and smaller noisemakers. The explosive festivities actually began weeks before the holiday, building to a crescendo on the 4th, and gradually tapering off until everyone used up their entire supply of fireworks.

On this particular Fourth of July, when I was perhaps ten, I heard that dog howling and I walked up to John's house. I was thrilled to see a beagle. "Why's he doing that?" I asked John. John looked at me with eyes that seem reminiscent of the ones that Mr. Wilson shoots at Dennis the Menace in the comic, if Mr. Wilson had been a lean, wiry man.

"I'm not sure," John shook his head, "He might be scared of the noise, but I don't think he is. Some guys have been hunting with him and said that he wasn't scared of the noise."

Whiskers threw his head back, as only a hound can do, ears flopped backwards, nose pointed skyward, a deep, monotone howl soaring to the clouds and beyond. I have heard many howls since then and to this day I have heard nothing that seems to approach it.

I have a dog, Rebel, that gives the saddest howl you ever heard when I leave him. My wife and I once took him on the road with us, hunting our way across a couple states and visiting family and friends from seminary. We spent two nights in a hotel that allowed dogs, and when we returned we had a complaint from the management that the dog howled while we were shopping for a few food items and soap. The dog is perfectly happy in the car though, because that is part of his home turf. We were going to walk to a restaurant a hundred yards from the hotel, but instead we loaded Rebel into the crate on the back seat, drove around the block, and left him in the car for an hour while we had supper. It was late November and pitch dark, but Reb sat happy in that car, sleeping on one of my hunting shirts, not even emitting one lonesome howl.

That is not the howl that Whiskers was making on that day 25+ years ago. I can still hear it, hanging in the air someplace, reverberating off the Alleghany Mountains through time. I don't think it was gun shyness. Nor do I think he was harking to a gun. Some people can't tell the difference, you know. I have a gutsy hound named Lady that will hark to a gun. She's a pretty good rabbit dog. I trialed her when she was young maybe a bit too much as a derby bitch. She was almost always in second series, although not always in western PA—she made Whiskers look like he was in slow motion. She backed into some winners' packs too. I have killed many rabbits in front of her, and I once made a practice of feeding her the hearts of the rabbits I shot. You do that a couple hundred times to a dog and they are conditioned. She knows *Boom* every bit as well as Whiskers knew "walk". I was at a trial one time when the judge fired the blank gun (to test for gun-shyness) while the dogs were on a long check. Lady blasted out of the brush towards the Judge, barking and jumping up on his leg.

"Gun-shy! Pick her up!" He yelled.

"What?" I asked, "That bitch has never been gun-shy a day in her life. She has eaten more rabbit meat than you have. They have been on check for almost five minutes— the pack either lost or holed the rabbit, you fired the gun and she took the direct line to what she thought was the bunny."

"What are you talkin' bout, harkin' to a gun?" the judge asked, "There ain't no such thing. Why, a gun and a dog don't sound nothing like one another."

"No, but that isn't why she runs to the gun. Haven't you ever had a dog get wise to the gun after enough hunting?" I questioned. He stared at me and blinked as if I was speaking a foreign language. I stopped Lady from touching the guy, just in case it was a contagious sort of stupid. "I think I better pick her up, I am not so sure that she would go any further under your scrutiny anyway." I went to the truck and socialized. I stayed for the duration of the trial, and would gladly describe the winners' pack from that day to you, but the rabbit never circled and the pack never moved far enough for anyone other than the judges and handlers to see the run. I still shudder to think that a judge, approved by a seminar to judge licensed trials, actually said, "What are you talkin' bout, harkin' to a gun? There ain't no such thing. Why, a gun and a dog don't sound nothing like one another."

On the other hand, I would love to fault that same hound for being over eager to run to a gun. She has tried to run to guns that were nowhere near us after long periods of finding no rabbits to chase. *C'est la vie*, as our northern friends would say, I have learned to live with the fault. As we near the Fourth of July, I am ready for Lady and her fits of hunting anxiety. She looks for rabbits after every firework boom. She jumps and barks wildly. She will spend the day in the basement, somewhat sheltered from the noise that she perceives to be the best rabbit hunt ever.

Come to think of it, maybe that is what Whiskers' howl represented. There was a famous Spanish Philosopher, Jose Ortega y Gasset who wrote on hunting. Actually, he got famous for writing on other topics, and most of the academics seem to ignore his book *Meditations on Hunting*. It is almost like the other philosophers are embarrassed that such a well-know colleague would write on hunting. But, I would like to give you the English translation of one of my favorite parts of the book, from a chapter about the addition that dogs brought to the ancient hunters who first utilized the canines in their hunting endeavors. He says:

> Here is the dog, which has always been an enthusiastic hunter on his own initiative. Thanks to that, man integrates the dog's hunting into his own and so raises hunting to its most complex and perfect form... There it is, there's the pack! Thick saliva, panting, chorus of jaws, and the arcs of tails excitedly whipping the countryside! The dogs are hard to restrain; their desire to hunt consumes them, pouring from eyes, muzzle, and hide. Visions of swift beasts pass before their excited eyes, while within they are already in hot pursuit.

I think I now know what the howl was that Whiskers made. He had hunted just enough to know the gun, or at least that is what I am willing to believe. He was experiencing that hot pursuit within but not the active running and pursuit on the outside of his body. His howl was half excitement and half regret. His ears told him that he was missing the best rabbit hunt ever, and there was nothing he could do about it. I wonder if that howl is preferable to having Lady bounce off the walls and furniture. I hope to have that conversation with John and Whiskers some day, both are long gone to eternal reward.

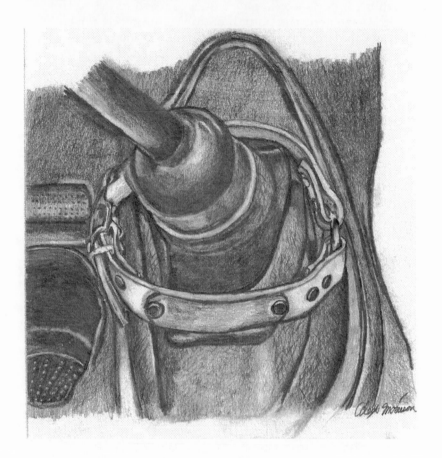

A SHORT ADVICE COLUMN

Many of our readers have asked me for advice, somehow feeling that as a clergyman I might have some tremendous insights into living life. Well, to be honest, I am more than flattered by this high regard for my opinion, especially considering the fact that most of the parishioners whom I have served feel that my area of expertise is somewhat limited. Nonetheless, I have gathered a few nuggets of advice that I can proffer to you as obtained in conversations with other beaglers.

One common issue of pastoral care that I often hear from beaglers is this one:

> *Rev. Ford, I live in (insert city name) and love to run hounds. Unfortunately, there seems to be little hope for me, as there are no wild places and brush here. My job moved me to the city, and I am just uncertain about how to train beagles.*
> *Sincerely, John P. City-Dweller.*

Well, John, I am uncertain what to offer you here. As I am sure you are aware, the Lord promised us all a cross to bear. Unfortunately, living in the city is one of the heaviest crosses to be handed out by the Almighty. Extreme sickness and physical suffering are, of course, worse than living in your city, but otherwise your cross ranks up there as one of the most difficult to bear. Cheer up though, it could be worse—some people have to live in New Jersey.

From James T. O'Brian:

> *Rev. Ford, Do you find it to be a good spiritual discipline to clean both barrels of your double barrel shotgun, even when blessed with such a fine day as to never dirty the second barrel.*
> *P.S. Do you want to hunt with me this fall?*

James, I have never had this problem myself—I tend to dirty both barrels, or none at all. I find killing the rabbit on the first shot to be unnecessary boasting, and this can lead to people not wanting to hunt with you. It is intimidating to hunt with a superb marksman. I, therefore, often miss intentionally on the first shot in order to make the second attempt more challenging. On many occasions I will miss with the second round as well, which tends to put the rabbit into a velocity that few can lead. My hunting partners like to tease me a bit about this, and my supposed "poor shooting ability." It does, however, keep them hunting with me. Naturally, cursing and complaining after missing twice helps to carry the façade of having erred. No one enjoys hunting with a vastly superior shooter. Oh, and Jim, I have no desire to hunt with you.

Here is a gem from Susan Grubbs:

> *Pastor, is there a prayer that you can recommend for the frustration that comes with trying to keep up with the dog hair that beagles shed? I brought a beagle into the house because I have read in your column that you find the beagle to be an excellent hunter and house pet as well.*

Indeed, Susan, the beagle makes a wonderful pet. The prayer I most commonly use is this one, "Oh Lord, what was I thinking when I brought these mutts in the house? All I do is vacuum and press tape to my clothing in order to remove the hair. Oh God, why is it that clerical shirts are black and show every tiny, white hair from the beagle? Please, Lord, inspire a genius to invent a tool that will solve shedding." By the way Susan, some prayers are unanswered.

Here is a common question, most recently asked by a new hunter named Joe Huntsman:

> *Rev. Ford, how many dogs do you tend to hunt with at a time? Do you think the Lord has a preference in this matter?*

Joe. I tend to hunt several ways. I often hunt with just one dog, especially if hunting hare. Rabbits tend to be easier targets with fewer beagles behind them, although this does not require one to brag by using only one barrel on their double gun (see Jim's question above). Certainly, running more beagles means more fun, and I am prone to take an entire pack when roads are not a big danger to the hounds. We have all been in a position where we have owned a dog that has trouble chasing a rabbit solo, and that dog needs the assistance of packmates. If you happen to have a whole kennel of dogs unable to solo, then I recommend that you jump into field trialing with both feet, success could be yours. I believe the Lord advocates a pack of hounds each capable of pounding a rabbit when hunted alone, otherwise they have nothing to offer to the pack.

Kimberly Jackson wrote:

Hey Preacher! I seem to shoot more rabbits than my husband, and I haven't hunted as long as he has. Why is this? Will it cause marital tension?

Funny you should ask. My wife and I experience this same phenomenon. As I often tell her, I allow her to do better than me to encourage her in the shooting sports. On several occasions she has challenged me to a contest, forcing me to shoot my best, and she still won. No doubt this is because she is closer to the ground where the rabbits are, and also due to the fact that I am taller than she, which consequently results in the sun always being in my eyes, even on overcast days while facing north. Marital tension only arises if you gloat about your better day in the field over the supper table. I provide free grief counseling to those men who have discovered that their wives are better hunters. For a nominal fee, I can arrange to have the firing pin altered to misfire in a wife's shotgun in order to decrease her success. It is a sinful thing, yes, but it provides opportunity for prayers of contrition and repentance, which God bids us to do. It also evens the odds.

Mike Archer asks:

Do you think it is a sin to hunt on the Sabbath?

Mike, I do not find it to be a sin. The Commonwealth of Pennsylvania, on the other hand, seems to think that varmint hunting is allowed on Sundays, but forbids all other hunting. If you live in a state that allows for hunting on Sundays, then you can praise God for such blessings. Naturally you should still go to church, and confine your hunting to afternoons on the Lord's Day. Saturday evening worship is also an option in some churches. Those of us in the Keystone State bear the cross of no Sunday hunting. Even so, it is a preferable cross to the sentence of living in New Jersey.

Jackson Clump wrote me as well, he asks:

Rev. Ford, I enjoy hunting hare and cottontail. Do you have a favorite recipe for hare?

Mr. Clump, I too hunt both. The white hare on white snow is unsurpassed for sporting pleasure—although shooting white hare on brown leaves seems a bit crass. As far as hare recipes, try this one: Cut the hare into pieces— four legs and the saddle. Season well with salt, and bring the meat to a slow boil. If it is particularly cold outside, it is nice to add some moisture into the house's air, and so I might let the hare boil all day. Don't add any more seasonings or vegetables to the hare. When the meat falls off the bone, turn off the heat and allow it to cool. While the hare is cooling, take your best beagle out and shoot a cottontail. Return home and cook the cottontail the way you like. Put the hare meat over Purina ONE (or your hound's favorite dog food) and throw the pot that held the hare away. Eat supper with your hound. Ha Ha. No, seriously Jackson, I eat a lot of hare and cottontail. I tend to think that the cottons taste better, but I like the hare just fine, but I use more garlic and pepper. And they are more fun to gun!

Last, but not least, is this query from Timothy Howe, who writes:

Mr. Ford, Are your beagles spoiled, and will a housedog hunt?

Tim, In fact a housedog will hunt, and do it well. I think they listen a little better, actually. On the other hand, they do tend to get too good of treatment and you worry more about roads and hazards with your pet than you do a potlicker who drives you nuts barking in the kennel. Spoiled? My dogs think that they own my 4x4 and howl when I go anywhere in it without them, they have full run of the house and have forced me to lock the refrigerator to prevent grand theft from the lunch meat drawer. My wife leaves the blinds in the living room open so that the hounds can bark at the neighbors as they walk their dogs, and I actually save coupons for dog treats. Oh, and I have been known to buy a ham hock for a beagle when they put forth a particularly valiant effort in the field—a little snack to eat in the crate on the way home. Unless the ham hock recipient is Rebel, who gets to sit in the passenger seat, and never rides in the crate. He likes to have the air conditioning on his face on those early-season, hot, fall afternoons. Is that spoiled?

Well, that is all the questions I have time for today. But you can send your future inquiries to me by email or U.S. postal service. Perhaps I can write another advice column in one of the beagle magazines. I wish good running to you, few checks, and full game bags. Leave a few for the next year.

How To Survive A Few Days In The City

For some of my readers, United Methodists may be a fairly unknown, mysterious lot. My Baptist friends tend to find Methodists to be a bit too sedate. "You guys nod your head 'yes' instead of shouting 'Amen!' for some reason," one fellow pastor once told me. On the other hand, a Presbyterian colleague thought that we Methodists were some of the most boisterous folks in any pews imaginable. I suppose each tradition has its own peculiarities, but I am sure that we are all worshiping the same God. But, if you ask me, the oddest thing that United Methodist do is this: They decide to wait until the weather is hotter than blazes —in June—and they hold a meeting that lasts several days. We call it the Annual Conference. There are lots of business matters and plenty of worship, and sometimes an argument or two.

Now, here is my dilemma at conference time. You see I have house hounds that are accustomed to running rabbits early in the morning and then lying around the house all day. What do I do with these mutts when I am away for 3-4 days? One year I left them with a friend who kenneled the beasts free of charge. It is very easy to move a kennel dog into a house; it is much harder to do the reverse. My dogs escaped by clawing and gnawing through the wooden door of the kennel, and it was very well built. My friend woke up to the sound of a trio of hounds scratching at his door and barking to get in!

During another Annual Conference I let the dogs stay at a church member's house, the family decided to have the beagles in their home to see if they really wanted to get a pet dog for themselves. I neglected to inform the family about the distinctly gluttonous appetite of beagles. My own home has a child lock on the refrigerator and no food is left on the kitchen table or at the edge of the counters. This has been the only real problem I have had with beagles in the house—they cannot be broken from stealing food—and they will endure any punishment for the most meager morsel. The host family for my beagles kept finding the dogs larger each morning and did not realize what was happening until they started finding empty bags of bread and scattered remnants of packaging lying around the corners of rooms. Have you ever seen a beagle after it eats a loaf of bread and then gulps a bowl of water?

I decided to spend the money and hire a professional kennel one year. It was an awesome facility—a large spacious kennel with exterior, concrete runs surrounded by two chain link fences. I knew that even my dogs would not be able to escape that incarceration system! You can imagine my surprise when the kennel called my cell phone and left a message, "Your dogs bark constantly. They sniff the wind and carry on at the top of their voices. I do not know what to do." Later, it was discovered that a large population of rabbits lived outside the chain link fences, and they ate clover all day and night. The rabbits could be scared away in daylight, but the owner of the kennel gave up trying to clear her property of rabbits. The beagles had to be quarantined inside the kennel shed during the night, sleeping in crates, inside a closet where they could not smell the dining rabbits in the yard.

Of course none of the options prepares any dog-sitter for the reality that my beagles wake up an hour before first light every single day and expect to go to the field for a chase. They are quite vocal about these expectations. I suppose I could just let someone run the dogs for a few days, but the animals are spoiled rotten, and I am picky about where I let them chase—no roads are permitted. I also do not like to let young dogs get beaten on the chase by older, more seasoned kennel mates (or, in this case, housemates). Oh sure, a good contest now and again is great, but no dog ever learned how to solve checks or run a good line by getting beat every day. I think there are bad habits in such practices. But, maybe a few days of this would not be so bad.

Oh, and there is the problem of my not knowing what to do during conference with myself. I am stuck in town and surrounded by all that cement and steel. I wake up early, as usual, and there are precious few rabbits to be found, much less a beagle. I wander around in the morning, hoping to hear a dog or maybe see a rabbit. Primarily, I hear cars and see buildings. June is the last month of the non-oppressive heat for the summer. The early mornings are still cool enough to really enjoy a good rabbit chase. I suppose that I am no easier on my fellow pastors than my hounds are on the kennel owners.

I hate to give the wrong impression about my tradition. It isn't as if I despise conference or anything. Parts of the week are quite enjoyable. Very often we import some fine preachers for the event. It is just the matter of city noise and long sessions that seem daunting to me. Perhaps I will try to locate one of the beagle clubs in the greater Harrisburg area and seek asylum within their running grounds. Maybe they will let a country preacher seek a bit of respite in the early morning hours on their running grounds before he goes into town for meetings, maybe even house a dog or two. Yes, perhaps that is the answer, I will sentence all the hounds but one to a kennel. One privileged hound could accompany me to make the days start smoothly. I belong to a denomination that had its origin in the backwoods and rolling hills. Methodism sprung up as a powerful movement in rural America.

That is still true of Methodists in many ways, although I fear that it might also be true that the denomination is not as romantic about those rural roots as I am. I sometimes think that people forget where food and lumber and all the building blocks of our society come from—out in the country where beaglers and beagles live. In many ways I might be living in the past, do you think? I'll have to think on this matter at conference. I do my best thinking with rolling hills and a rolling bawl from an enthusiastic beagle serving as background music. What is the future for people like myself? I will require a hound to help me ponder these things. I wonder if the Bishop will notice my boots.

ARTISTIC APPRECIATION AND BUREAUCRACY

I have to confess that I have always had an appreciation for the arts. Well, I should say that I have always appreciated an artistic firearm. There is something about a beautiful shotgun that makes hunting seem better. Firstly, there is something about an American shotgun that makes me stand right up and get a bit patriotic about hunting. Why do so many turn an eye across the Atlantic when looking for a good shotgun. Nothing against those European firearms, but a Fox or an Ithaca makes my spirit soar.

Lest I forget, I am partial to the double barrels. Please don't tell me how effective your 3" autoloader with the plastic stock is on everything from turkey to rabbit. I know. I know. Please don't tell me that sometimes the third shot is just what was needed. I know. I know. I have seen others do just this very thing. Truthfully, I almost always kill my rabbit or odd beagle-flushed-bird on the first shot. That isn't a boast either. It just seems that if I miss on that first attempt then the second will naturally fail too. Oh, and when I use my pump gun, I will miss on the third shot as well. A third shot on a running rabbit moving further out of range has rarely been beneficial to me. It is as if my number of shots is inversely proportional to my success rate. I rely heavily on that first attempt, and the second try will only sometimes pay off. The tighter choke on the second barrel has always seemed better to me than two more of the first shot. Sometimes my one good shot is made with the second barrel if the rabbit is a bit further away.

Again, I know that the record will prove me wrong. One of my best hunting buddies uses a Mossberg autoloader 12 gauge. He owns no hounds and shoots at turkey in the spring and rabbits in the fall with me—no other shotgunning—no grouse, no squirrel, no pheasant, no woodcock, no hare, and no second season rabbits. Every time we go out, he shoots more rabbits than I do in front of my hounds! He shoots more often than I do, but even so I also know he has more range. His gun can reach out and tumble a rabbit with more consistency at 45 yards than my shotguns. I would never shoot that far with my guns. His second and third shots often pay dividends.

But, that is another peculiarity about the arts that I appreciate. I like older guns, the ones that our fathers and grandfathers used. My favorite is not inherited, but it is from the same era. It is an A.H. Fox made in 1927. Many of these older guns are chambered 2 ½" and cannot use the 2 ¾" shells that are normally found on the shelves of today's sporting goods stores that are staffed with people who know little about hunting or the tools that are used for hunting. If you ever want to be entertained, ask a Wal-mart or *Dick's Sporting Goods* employee about hunting equipment. I once had this conversation in one of these stores:

"Say, you wouldn't happen to have any 2 ½" shells for older guns would ya?"

"Like, how old are ya talkin'? Way back in the 1980's?"

"Ah, no, older than that. Is there anyone here that actually hunts and shoots?"

"I shoot paintball every week."

That was when I decided to stop looking for anything that I really need in a store that ends in "mart" or sells more golf clubs than hunting gear. Fortunately there are still some places that make shells for the older, more classic guns. I believe I have mentioned the Polywad Company in another article. They make ammunition. Their stuff is tops and they can get you shells for the shotguns chambered 2 ½". I am fortunate enough to live close to Lion Country Supply, and can stop in and purchase Polywad shells anytime. They have a spreader load that is awesome—an overused word—at short range. These loads are very effective in the first season when the rabbits are darts in the weeds. The spreader loads open quickly for great coverage at close distances.

I also appreciate rare art. Rare art can mean a 16 gauge. My friends think I ought to go to a 12 or a 3" 20. I resist their advice and try to ignore the taunts as I walk into the brush with a side-by-side 16. I am very partial to 16s. I don't know why. I just seem to hit well with them. And they seem so much lighter than a 12. I have never been a fan of carrying a real heavy gun all day when you are only allowed to shoot a few rabbits. Four is our limit per day in Pennsylvania. I have seen how light the synthetic stock autoloaders are. I know. I know. But my Fox is only 6 pounds. It swings fast and I do well when I take it out. My 16 gauge *Fox* with Polywad spreader shells is a very fine team at ranges from very close to 35 yards. If the rabbits are staying further away than 35 yards then my buddy has to tumble them with his autoloader with turkey loads. If he isn't with me then the dogs have to circle it again—which isn't all bad either. The 16 hits hard and doesn't leave you trying to clean rabbits that are more shot than bunny. It is light to carry and I like the wooden stock. Of course finding brushes and cleaning equipment can be hard, but it is still possible to find equipment for 16 gauges. I avoid the "marts."

So those are my artistic leanings—American, double barrel, older, 16 gauge shotguns. I don't encounter them very often. But here is the thing—every time I do, I have an expired driver's license. This is true! It is no doubt hotter than Hades at the moment that you read this in August, but I happened to come across a piece of hunting art in June. It was a side-by-side 16 gauge. A Lefever made in 1930. Now Lefever was the first to introduce the hammerless double barrel, but the company eventually came to be owned by Ithaca, who produced the Nitro Special that I bought.

You can imagine my disappointment when I tried to buy the gun only to discover that my driver's license had been expired since February! It gets worse, the same thing happened to me in June of 2005, when I bought my Fox. In both instances I had to go to the Department of Motorized Vehicles to renew my license before I could acquire the beautiful 16 gauges. I am not sure how your home state works, but in Pennsylvania the standard practice is to have just one camera capable of taking the necessary photograph for the license. This one camera often works improperly. This camera, when it does work, is capable of producing one photograph in 3.5 minutes. Although I feel that some user error may be involved here. How do I know this? I timed it. There were 23 people ahead of me in line. The DMV itself provided all sorts of entertainment. People were coming from out of state and seeking a PA driver's licenses. Some folks were registering vehicles, or trying to do so. Others wandered in and asked to get vehicles inspected. Garages do this service, not the DMV, and this caused great confusion and a few arguments.

In short, this was a very stressful place. Add to this the occasional delay in the photographer's work due to an inability to remove a glare from the eyeglasses or for someone wanting to go backwards in the process to make themselves an organ donor or to remove themselves from organ donation status, and the end result is about fifty taxpayers (at any given moment) waiting in a room full of fold out chairs who are ready to explode. By contrast, there were the employees of the DMV who lived in such chaos every day. They were accustomed to incompetence, confusion, and the many layers of state bureaucracy that tended to make everything much harder than it had to be. I considered explaining to an employee how important it was for me to buy this Lefever before the store closed, but then I realized that one of two things would happen. One, the employee could go mental at the mention of the word "gun" and go into some sort of Department of Homeland Security training. I almost encountered such a thing when I had to procure a real Social Security card a year or so ago. I was teaching some introductory college course and had to have a genuine copy of my Social Security card in order to be hired. Naturally, I did not have such a card and had to go to the Social Security office to get one issued. When I entered the office, I was greeted by a gentleman in uniform (I think he worked for The Department of Homeland Security, but I can't remember). He asked standard questions, the last of which was, "Are you armed?"

"No," I said.

"Do you have a pocketknife?"

"Yeah," I answered.

"Then you're armed! Leave the knife here while you talk to the clerk."

Now, if my pocketknife was that bad at the Social Security office (which was mostly empty), then I wasn't even going to mention the fact that I wanted to buy a shotgun at the pressure cooker environment of the DMV. Someone might misunderstand and think I said that I had one with me or something. Of course, the other thing that might have happened was that I could have talked about the beautiful find of this old double barrel Lefever, made in Ithaca New York, and the beauty of having it with my Fox and the fact that I could use the same shells in both guns, and how nice this would be with my hunting hounds and a day in the field. No doubt, had I done this, the DMV employee would have been as non-appreciative as the Wal-Mart kid who likes to shoot paintball guns.

So, I waited. I went out to my truck and returned some phone calls. I ran into town and got a Pepsi. I did some work on the sermon that was due in a few days. It was all strangely reminiscent of that day four years previous when I brought home the Fox. Eventually the DMV locked the doors. No kidding. Those of us who were inside could finish, but no new customers were entering. The line moved at the same gruelingly slow pace. Once it even went backwards as the woman calling out numbers accidentally called numbers that were processed 45 minutes earlier. Eventually she determined that no one was coming to the front because she was in error, not because people had left. When she finally returned to where she had left, off she skipped a person who was right in front of her and that caused another delay.

Then it was my turn. I wondered if this is how my Bavarian ancestors must have felt when they arrived here in the 1800's—certainly their impatience was greater after having traversed the ocean, but I was mighty frustrated after having stood in a long line that enabled me to sit in yet a longer line. I stood up and walked to the front, my backside sore from sitting. I was asked to verify my address many times. It seemed like at least 13 times. I was asked to register to vote if I had not been registered. I was asked to donate my organs. I was asked to sit for a picture. I was asked if the picture was good enough! "The picture is fine," I said, "I am not going to hang it on the wall for company to see. I am going to shove it in my wallet and sit on it every day that I have it." The older lady working the photography machine laughed, handed me my license, and then called out a number she had called out 20 minutes earlier. I exited the DMV through the doors that were designated for leaving after the entrances were locked and managed to buy the Lefever just before the store closed.

So how is the gun? It is just fine. The barrels are two inches longer than the Fox, and it weighs just a bit more. I shot some clays and it fits me well. I knew it would, or rather, I would have fooled myself into thinking it did, had it not. What do I do when the first day of rabbit season comes around? I have two different American made, double barrel, older, 16 gauge shotguns. Do I flip a coin? Take the Ithaca pump instead? Maybe I should confuse my friends and bring the 12 gauge. Well, I have to buy my new hunting license soon. I hear that this year the whole process will be done electronically, using the driver's license. No more paper applications. No doubt I will have a bureaucratic line of sufficient length to think through this new dilemma. At least my driver's license is current.

A FRIEND RETURNS

Autumn is here. What a wonderful time of year. In the early rabbit season there is a sacred feeling to those days that begin with frost and visible breath and end in sun soaked afternoons that make you think it might be August if not for the fact that dusk arrives so much earlier and the leaves are showing their dazzling colors. My hounds are getting into top shape from the lazy summer. It always seems odd to me that I lose weight when the mercury rises and my beagles pack it on. They run sporadically in the hottest months, and those trips afield are short in duration. The humidity and soaring temperatures have no effect on the ravenous beagle appetite, and the beasts frequently find a way to steal food and gorge themselves in the corners of the fenced lawn. The only evidence of these crimes is a shredded pretzel bag or empty pack of hamburger buns blowing across the yard in the breeze.

To be sure, sometimes the crime is heard, especially if the absconded food is large enough to create a fight, or more accurately, a growl fest. These events are loud and sound more violent than they really are. More often than not, however, the culprit acts alone and is visibly swollen from an appetite that knows no bounds. The massive beagles will then retreat to the basement and smash their bulging stomachs against the cool cement. Such is the life of the house dwelling hunting beagle in the hot summer heat.

Autumn represents a transformation. These pudgy basement beagles are lean and fit. Even if culinary thefts continue, the increased exercise of autumn makes such infractions mostly harmless in terms of metabolic activity, as the extra calories are readily utilized in pursuit of cottontails. The calendar is in a place that lends itself to great days. My truck will have a bit of luggage in the back. Brush pants and boots will live in the vehicle until after small game season ends. I become a bit delinquent in my duties as I sneak into some hunting grounds. It would not be uncommon to find me at a late morning meeting wearing dew dampened boots on my feet while a beagle slept in the bed of the truck, only slightly distracted by the hunting vest that still has enough rabbit odor for the dog to notice. The day's meat typically sits inside a cooler on the floor of the passenger side of the truck.

It is also during fall that I might be seen hurrying to the brush piles and delaying supper until after sunset. Oh, I will be reprimanded for missing supper a few times. The porch light will get a bit more use as I sit out in the chilled night air and clean rabbits. Apples are in season too and I am forever stuffing plastic grocery bags of the fruit into my game vest for my wife to prepare desserts. Black walnuts are around as well, and when crushed they make a tremendous "breading" for baked rabbits.

I never use an alarm clock—I tend to rise early, but the autumn months seem to exaggerate this tendency. I drink coffee early and daydream myself awake to thoughts about where to hunt. I try to wake early enough to allow time to drive wherever I might choose, and be there at first light.

Autumn makes me a child again. I get anxious to hunt. I might even have trouble getting to sleep the night before. I may actually pout when it rains. Once in a while I will even hunt in the rain if I feel it might pass soon. I hunted in the drizzling drain all the time as a kid. I prefer to not do so now, but the end of October and beginning of November can persuade me that I am a teenager again. I hope to see some of you out hunting this year. Someday, I would like to hunt swamp rabbits, jackrabbits, or maybe the European hare. Maybe some other autumn...

This autumn will soon find me cleaning a shotgun every night by the fireplace. Sure, it might not be quite cold enough for a roaring fire in October, but I will have one anyway. I can crack the window. People who know me can see happiness taking root within me. Some may ask why? Well, let me introduce you to the reason. Ladies and Gentlemen, it is my pleasure to present to you...Autumn. Welcome back dear friend.

BACK TO SCHOOL

School is back into swing. This has always marked serious changes in my life as a beagler. Dating back to middle school, things have always become profoundly different when the calendar year turns towards autumn. Things still change for us, and we must learn to adapt. As a kid the fall was the hope of a new hunting season mixed with regret over the prospect of having to endure sitting in a classroom for 7 hours (Was it that long?) every weekday.

On the bonus side was the fact that I got new sneakers. Now I never liked new sneakers, but every school year began with a new pair of sneakers. The first day of school always smelled like a *Sears and Roebuck* store because of the new shirts and new blue jeans. I began school in the late seventies when such a dress code had replaced more formal attire. The halls echoed with the sound of sneakers squeaking loudly with every step on their new soles. But the old sneakers, ah, that was where the joy was—they could now be used to play outside! Those old sneakers, which were still in pretty good shape, were perfect for chasing beagles in the evening. They were great in the morning dew too, but your feet got soaked. It would be years before I could afford a pair of feather light boots. My feather light boots were a pair of dirty but structurally sound sneakers. As I recall the high top sneakers were common, even though very few played basketball. No matter, the shoes were great for ankle-support in the woods and fields as well.

Oftentimes I would run in from school, change into my old sneakers, and leash a dog or two to walk up the hill behind the house for a chase. There weren't many rabbits up that hill, but they were all woods rabbits that ran hard and far, so hard that sometimes I looked for signs that the dogs were running a deer because of the size of the circles that were more like squares—few checks and long straight drives. But when the chase proved true to the quarry, and a rabbit was verified as the lead of the show, I would relax and watch the pursuit. Usually I remembered to change my good shirt as well as my shoes. Sometimes I would forget, and the school shirt would get muddy, or worse, torn. The pants always withstood the woods fine, although an occasional briar hole might appear. There were days when I returned and tried to wash my clothes before mom saw the dirt.

But the chases were not as good as the morning ones, and I was no longer able to run rabbits in the morning because of school. Oh sure, I would sneak out for a few pre-school morning runs, but that never lasted long. All I had to do was be late for school once due to the dogs, and not only was I incarcerated in the classroom, but I had my beagle privileges revoked too. Ah, and the evening runs had to end early for homework. The rabbits were just getting active when I had to go home. The school year was hard on a young beagler.

Hey, it is no easier now. I have a stepson in the house that requires Herculean efforts to arouse from slumber and send out the door to the bus. Being a stepfather, I sometimes lack the sound parenting skills that are needed for these tasks. "Why don't we just pour water on him," I suggested to my wife.

"No! You can't do that, no father would do that," She replied.

"Mine did," I rebutted, remembering the moment, "Once. He did it once. I always woke up pretty good after that."

Alas, no, we live in an age where kids have no chores (How many of you also had to carry firewood after school before you could play?) no work ethic, no responsibility, and no fear of a morning bath via a glass of water before the morning shower. I still remember my dad saying, "Now that you're up, put those wet sheets in the washing machine." I knew how to do it too, because I had been washing school clothes that got dirty running dogs before mom knew they were dirty. By the time my wife and I get Wes ready for school, the prime beagling hour is almost over. I don't know how bealglers with multiple kids in the house function!

Oh, and lest I forget, there is the school bus, or should I say buses. There are millions of these things, many equipped with drivers that, it seems to me, no one else would hire. Every hundred feet the bus stops and one kid slowly walks out of his house and meanders in the most time consuming way to his bus. One hundred feet later the process repeats itself, only this time the kid forgets something and has to go back into the house, taking even more time. When did this insane process start? I remember when the bus stopped only once or twice in each neighborhood. It didn't matter if the bus went by your house en route to the school; everyone was herded into central locations so that the bus would stop a handful of times and be full! You played touch football while waiting for the bus, and sometimes got grass stains on your knees as you caught a low pass while trying to keep your feet in bounds. Nowadays I follow buses, stopping behind them constantly, people looking at me as if I am crazy because of the barking hounds in the truck looking for a rabbit. I am trying to get to the woods and these kids are filling the seats one or two at a time. As I creep behind the bus, I pray for a good, old-fashioned farm family to be the next stop, for an entire squad of kids to emerge from one house and for them to fill the bus to the gills. But no, the only way to get to the brush in less than 40 minutes is to leave before the fleet of yellow behemoths leave for their morning sorties—and in the hills of rural Pennsylvania they leave early.

Winter is even worse. I remember when, as kids, we walked outside and awaited the bus in freezing temperatures and shivered and shook. I recall arriving at school with frozen hair because I had to rush into the bathroom just before bolting out the front door—my sister took hours in the bathroom each morning, leaving me only seconds to wash up before school. There is no such inconvenience today. These days the few kids who do have to board the bus some distance from their house do not get cold. They await their school chariot from a warm car with a parent. As the bus pulls up, it takes an eternity for the child to emerge from the car and enter the bus. Kids once boarded the bus faster in the winter. You stand in the cold air with frozen hair and you will pass people to get onto that bus!

Oh, but who am I to grumble. Sure the summer is over and it is back to school for everyone. That can be sad, especially for those of us who are in school or teaching. And yes, I would like to avoid buses easier and be able to tune up my hounds in this September morning dew without all the traffic slowing my trip afield. All of that aside, it is the cusp of autumn. Leaves are changing. The air is cooler. Soon the smell of a wood fire will fill the air as homes gear up for winter. Can't you hear the sound of the axe as somebody splits the firewood that he should have split earlier? Of course you don't, everyone rents log splitters these days. Still, I can smell apples in the fields and the kitchen smells great as I preserve the rest of the garden—yes, I still can garden produce in jars and always will. My eyes see the grass in the yard as it stands strong, knowing full well it will soon fade and not grow until Spring. I smile at the lawn as I think, "Good bye oh chore of summer, the lawn mower will sit in blissful idleness while your green fades to yellow and goes dormant under white snow. The quickened days of the fall await and soon we will hunt." The hounds look at me differently, and not just because I am talking to the lawn. They are just a little fat from August. They spent much of that humid month sprawling their pudgy bellies into the cement floor of the basement—very few chases in August. Our time is here now, and I swear that these dogs know it. They know it very well. Heck, I have one dog that will bring a leash to me, telling me that it is time to go! It is a good thing that they know. Because at this time of year things get busy—at home, at school, in the church. We all need a few good beagles to remind us to celebrate autumn. Oh, and for what it is worth, during the fall hunting season, I wear *gore-tex* feather light boots in the morning—and sneakers in the afternoon—I feel faster in the sneakers as I climb hilly meadows and follow eager hounds that search for a rabbit to run.

BLACKBERRIES

What a difference a generation makes. It becomes more and more clear to me every day that I belong to a generation that is no longer really "with it" when it comes to the world today.

"I'm ready for some blackberries," I said to a group at the church.

"One blackberry should be enough for you, Pastor!" a young man responded.

"One? Are you nuts?" I replied, "I need thousands of them."

"Hope you have lots of money to buy them." Came a response from parishioners.

"Nah, I don't buy blackberries. I go get them for free," I said.

At this pronouncement a chorus of excitement erupted and everyone screamed, "Can I have one?"

"Sure," I said and I walked over to my vehicle, returning with a handful of berries, one for each congregant.

"What's this?" one interrogated.

"It's a blackberry," I pointed out the obvious, "You just asked for one. *Shheesh.*"

At this point everyone began to explain to me how a blackberry was really some kind of electronic device that, I think, sends and receives email. Apparently all present believed I had received free electronic equipment. Little do they know that electronic things have a severe reaction to me that several mechanics, two electricians and one home appliance repairman can only describe as "uniquely odd, bizarre, and uncanny."

Blackberries, on the other hand, the real ones, are something that I do know a thing or two about. My grandmother was the kind of person that you might try to avoid during the blackberry season. She had buckets fashioned from big coffee cans for each grandchild, and if she could locate you she would force you out into the underbrush and demand that you fill the can to the brim with good tasting berries. And she would hunt you down at your friend's house and force you out the door, banished from her sight until you met your quota. She was stern, strict, and would have made the nastiest Egyptian taskmaster seem polite. Once I could have sworn I heard her say that she was going to "issue bigger buckets and take away our carrying handles."

It was so bad on some days in August that as a teenager I would volunteer to go to my uncle's farm and make hay so as to get out of the berry duty—now that is just sad (and itchy). But, the year I was fifteen, I was saved from my weary labor by finding some huge blackberries— big as thumbs and wild as nature herself. Actually, that is a lie—my beagles found them. I only had two hounds then, Duke and Princess, and we hit the brush as much as we could. One day we had fantastic chases and rabbits that ran great and stayed above ground. And as I looked around me I saw these massive shade berries. It only took a small bit of time to fill that pail.

It all went well—the dogs and I left at dawn and chased some bunnies. Before midmorning and the worst heat arrived, I was walking home with dogs tugging leashes and a can full of my labor to deposit at the house. Then I had to start lying. You see, gram picked her quota of berries for the pantry too. And when I dumped mine into the sink for washing, she was pressing me as to where I got those berries. Now, I could walk you to the very spot those berries came from, even all these years later; but there was no way that I was revealing the location—because then everyone else would have been able to fill their cans fast and I would be back to rummaging all morning to meet my MDA (mandated daily allowance)

So when asked where the berries came from, I simply said, "Hmm. In the woods while walking, somewhere." Day after day the voices of those beagles bounced off those hills and day after day I was the first to return with my berries and beagles.

Then, one evening, grandma walked out the door with a five-gallon bucket and said she was going to pick berries as big as the ones I was bringing in. "Good luck," I said, "I wish I could describe where I got them."

"Oh, I'll find them," she said, and let my beagles out of the kennel. They streaked through the yard, across the alley, and over the hill. Grandma followed behind, much slower of course. She heard the chase and moved in that direction until she found the mother lode of blackberry heaven. "You can pick your dogs up anytime you want, I'm too old to chase after them," she said to me after filling the bucket almost half full. Her fingers were fast and accurate as they stripped the bushes of their berries. "I'll bring your sister and cousins back here tomorrow to pick the rest. You don't have to bother with that tomorrow. You just take those dogs of yours and find another place like this one." And that is how it went for the last couple weeks of blackberry season, with me and the dogs finding berries and my not having to pick very many. Some cousins were a little mad at me. But those dogs ate rabbit tracks every day and the preserves from that winter were the sweetest I had ever had before—or since.

BRAG HOUND

November has a tendency to excite me. It is by far my favorite month. My best days afield always seem to be in November, and there is no reason to doubt that this year will be any different. Big game hunting is still king in Pennsylvania, and deer season will produce the annual fiasco of way too many people (most of them hunters who only hit the woods a few days/year), jostling for way too small of a space. State game lands will become full of city-dwellers looking for that monster buck, and the private property will be characterized by hunters trespassing and feigning surprise whenever someone approaches and says, "Pardon me, but you are trespassing."

Small game season is my speed. No one is on the public grounds, mostly; and landowners are eager to give permission to the rabbit hunter. Thanksgiving dinner will be heavy on rabbit, grouse, pheasant and maybe some trout. November is the perfect month. It has always been that way for me. I had one of those fathers that never minded a boy skipping school for a day to hunt rabbits, so long as grades did not suffer. Times have changed—kids have a very difficult time missing school for any reason other than severe illness, and I shudder to think what would happen if a young hunter drove himself to school with a shotgun in the truck for an after school trip to a grouse cover that lay between the school and home. Wow, it seems hard to believe that we did that with no complaints or troubles. Simpler times.

November is also the source of my most harrowing trip afield with hounds. I wasn't old enough to drive and I managed to skip school on a Wednesday because Dad was off work then too. I can't tell you the details of the schedule, but my father changed shifts every week, rotating backwards from the 7-3 shift, to the 11-7, and lastly 3-11 before starting all over again. In addition, the day off changed too. Sometimes he was off on a weekend like many people tended to be scheduled, but it was rare. He might be off on any given day. The whole schedule was a mystery to me. The night before we went hunting, Dad was in a conversation with a friend about who had the dog with the better nose. Dad always favored our Princess who did well in poor conditions, even if she was a bit mouthy in high scent. Dad said, as he hung up the phone with his friend who had to work the next day, "Tomorrow Princess will prove her nose."

So, bright and early on a Wednesday we headed into the brush. It did not take long to bag a bunny, and then a second. Dad sat lighting his pipe while I field dressed a rabbit. The two dogs, Duke and Princess, struck a line and starting moving straight out of hearing.

"Deer?" I asked

"Yep," Dad bit his pipe, his mind half curious and half angry about the prospect of his dogs running a deer. The chase ran out over the flats and into the ferns and big timber. We never had a rabbit go out there.

"Better get ready to run," Dad tapped out his pipe and placed it in his pocket. He started jogging behind the dogs, or at least in the direction he thought they might have gone. I followed and we paused at the top of the hill. No sounds.

"You circle left, I'll circle right," Dad said.

I ran fast, pausing periodically to let the sound of the dry leaves under my boots subside so I could listen for hounds on the chase. I finally heard them. They were coming towards me! I stood still waiting to see a deer running through the trees. It should have been ahead of the dogs and I could cut the trail. The hounds became louder and clearer. I could hear Duke's high shrill over Princess's rolling bawl. And then they stopped. A long silence ensued and then they struck the line again, this time heading out away from me. I chased but could not keep up. At the top of the next rise I saw Dad.

"It's a fox," he said as he caught his breath, "Red fox."

"What do we do?" I asked.

"Try to get in front of the damn thing without it knowing," Dad answered. We tried for hours. The fox always moved out away, adjusting its circle to stay far from us. I saw it once, well over a hundred yards in front of me, crossing a dirt road. Dad finally appeared again and asked me to go wait at his deer stand. He told me that his plan was to go even further from there. He told me to stay still once I got there. We were very far from any place that we ever hunted rabbits! I was standing on Dad's stand for an eternity when he walked up to me. He had the heaviest beagle, Duke, in his game vest. He was carrying Princess. Both dogs had pads bleeding on their feet. The air was cold, and blasts of hot canine pants poured into the chilling air. Duke's head hung out of the hunting vest and fog seemed to envelope my father from the dog's heavy breathing.

"How did you get them?" I asked. I was 14 or 15 years old, and I held back the emotions that I was feeling an hour earlier. At that time I was sure that I would never see those dogs again!

"I had you here to turn the fox on this side, and I turned it into the coalmines from the other side. They were still chasing up there, but slow enough that I could catch them. Duke was pooped out and just following Princess as she walked that fox trail across the shale."

The old coalmine predated any sort of environmental awareness. It was mostly rock, a bit of vegetation but not much. Here and there a pine had taken root. It was mined at a time before coal companies were required to save the topsoil or replace the surface with green vegetation. My legs were tired from running, and we had a long walk to the truck. I put Princess in my game vest. Neither dog could run for weeks. They healed, but their paws were raw for some time. It was my worst November. I hope you never have this experience. I saw the fox just once during that chase; father saw it several times. It was never in shotgun range, and a rifle shot would not have been easy. That fox glided through the brush. How could something that red hide so well?

We aren't sure how long the chase lasted. It was dark when we got home, and the fox run started fairly early in the morning. Granted, the walk to the truck was well over an hour. We got home and took care of the dogs. Dad and I sat on the back porch and soaked our two rabbits in water. He puffed his pipe and smiled. I could not imagine what he was smiling about. He looked at me and said, "It takes a helluva good nose to run a fox across rocks." He always could see silver linings.

CHORES

For my money, there are no better times of the day than the first few hours of daylight and the last few hours before sunset. These are the times when I have taken most of the game that I have harvested—be it big game or small. Furthermore, I am in a position to be able to hunt those hours. I shepherd a flock that not only allows me to do that, but also encourage it, because they feel it makes me more effective as a pastor for them. So, a typical fall day may look like this: hunt from dawn until 9:00 a.m., work until suppertime (then skip supper), hunt until sunset, and then work 'till 10:00 p.m.

In the winter I may hunt from 3:00 –5:00 p.m. If it is a warm December, I may choose to hunt the first couple hours of daylight instead. Skipping supper can cause marital tension, but it is not every night and it isn't all year.

This brings me to the point of this essay—when you work full-time and hunt part-time, there are things that do not get tended. The tasks that are not completed are by and large chores that I am sure plague all sportsmen. For instance, the lawn is a classic example. I have never understood the desire to keep a perfectly mowed lawn. In my opinion, all true sportsmen know the following things about cutting the grass: First, when the yard is so shaggy as to stall out the mower, it is remarkable how much better it will mow if you pull the mower backwards over the lawn, rather than pushing the machine forwards. Second, when the height of your grass gets too high to mow backwards, you simply mow forward while "doing a wheelie" with the front end off the ground, and then run back over that same path using the aforementioned backwards mowing procedure. Please note that I am not advocating the "wheelie" method here, as I am sure it is dangerous—I am just saying that I have done it—and I am sure other sportsmen have as well.

Leaves. Who, in this world, has time to rake leaves? I would no sooner rake leaves than I would mow my grass twice each week—and I have lots of neighbors who do both. So, you may ask, what do I do about leaves? I'll tell you. My poor lawn mower has a hard life. It spends all summer going backwards and riding wheelies. So, to show my appreciation, I let it have one easy ride in the fall, after all the grass is dead and short and the leaves are stacked high, I simply mow the leaves and let the winter winds scatter their veined remains to the well manicured lawns to my southeast. Ha-ha. Sure, a few twigs might nick the mower blade, but that's nothing compared to the things that get run over in the high grass.

Snow removal. Here is how I handle the early, light snows: I treat them with the philosophy that God put the snow there, and he will take it away. I postpone shoveling that snow as I walk the dog and shotgun to the vehicle. Sure enough, in a day or two the sun melts it down. As for the snow that won't leave until spring: Here we are in a bit of a dilemma. There was a time when I paid kids to remove this snow. Alas, kids today can only be found hypnotized by video games and television screens. They have given up on going outside and doing anything. I have even heard reports that children in New Jersey have been inside for so much of the day, for so many generations, that the kids there are born eyeless like subterranean newts.

So, here is what I do—I postpone snow removal until everything gets shut down for a day. Schools close, and the weatherman says that everyone is to stay home. Then I go out and shovel. But here is the catch—you can't shovel old snow that has been walked upon. So, as you procrastinate on the snow removal you must walk beside your sidewalk, in the lawn, so as to not compress the snow and make ice. If you do compress the snow with your footsteps, you are in trouble and will have to actually work hard.

As for the driveway snow, I use my 4X4 to tramp down a runway. This then creates a path for both my four-wheel drive hunting rig, as well as my wimpy car. As the winter progresses, I find my long driveway being transformed into a luge. Going down I find it harder to stop as the winter intensifies, and coming home requires more of a running start to make it. Don't laugh; I am sure that there are other beaglers out there who know exactly what I am talking about.

Weeding the garden is another difficult chore to find time for. I always plant a big garden, but then do not want to weed it. Now, I will confess that I do weed regularly until the vegetables take hold, and then I just let the weeds come. Sure, I have to hunt for produce a little, but I have just as much in the garden bed as folks who weed every day. If anything, it is a pleasant surprise to pull back a wad of weeds and find a massive melon. I simply tell people I am being biblical in my gardening and I cite the Gospel reference to the wheat and tares as proof that this is not only an acceptable form of agriculture but also a divinely sanctioned one. Visitors to my garden leave believing that I am a reflective, contemplative horticulturalist rather than a lazy gardener.

I make no apologies. My vocation of pastoral ministry comes first, and then my out-of-doors pursuits come second. If my lawn is shaggy, well who cares? If my snow removal is tardy or nonexistent then so be it. I only have a two-foot long sidewalk. I garden for food, not pictures. I stand defiant against all that the neighbors might say or think. Although I have become more domestic since I got married some years ago. The wild in me may be forced out and I might have to not only mow the grass, but also do it in nice, picturesque patterns. I may buy a snow blower just to stay on top of the task of removing the white stuff. Nah, my Nay is a bright woman. She knows my limitations and she will never make me toe that kind of line. I am my own man and I ca-. Hold on, I gotta go, my beloved calls.

HOW TO PROPERLY
DIRTY A FINE SHOTGUN
AND ENJOY THE CLEANING

The phone rang. I answered it. "I got rust on my gun," Lenny said, "Rust. I can't believe it. I gotta start cleaning my guns more often. I just hate to do it."

"Yeah, it is something of a hard thing to do before November. But November marks the beginning of the enjoyable gun cleaning season," I said.

"Enjoyable? You're outta yer mind. I make my kid clean the guns. That's what kids are for. Dontch'ya remember when we had to clean all the guns? We cleaned our fathers' guns and our own too. Heck, it was expected of us in return for getting to go to the field." I said nothing in response. Lenny got nervous and after a long pause added, "Well, tell me I am right!"

"You are right, we used to clean guns for our dads...."

"And?" Lenny asked.

"Whaddya mean?"

"You always have an 'and' or a 'but', so what is it?"

"Neither. No 'and'. No 'but'," I said.

"Oh," Lenny replied, "You usually have to add an 'and' or a 'but'...."

"However," I interrupted, "That doesn't appear to be true anymore."

"What makes you say that?" Lenny groaned.

"Is there rust on your gun?" I asked.

"Yes."

"Was your kid supposed to clean your gun?" I continued.

"Yes." Lenny grumbled.

"Is there rust on his gun too?" I concluded.

"There better not be, that little 20 gauge was my father's gun!" I heard big booming noises as Lenny ran across his house. I heard him fumbling with locks and doors. "AHH! It's rusted too!" Lenny lamented.

"Say Lenny, better check that deer rifle he used last year in the rain," I said. He hung up shortly after that. Later on that week, we discussed the matter over a morning excursion to the brush with the dogs for a hunt.

"So, how did you know that the guns weren't cleaned by the kid," Lenny asked.

"I live with one. And I see many others around town and in church. Kids don't do the things that we did. If we make them mow the lawn they call it child abuse. They don't weed gardens or pick the vegetables. Naturally, they don't eat vegetables unless they are in a bag and called potato chips or corn chips. They don't feed animals, milk cows, bail hay, or even play outside!"

"Are you serious?" Lenny half-chuckled.

"Yeah, I am serious. When is the last time you saw kids playing outside unless it was for a school sport?"

Lenny scratched his head. I continued my questions, "Have you seen a group of kids playing catch? How about a pick-up game of football? When is the last time you saw a kid riding a bicycle rather than adults pedaling dressed up as if they were in the *Tour de France*? Is there a store that even sells sandbox toys for little kids? "

"My gosh, you're right. What do kids do?" Lenny panicked.

"Mine knows how to set the clock in the vehicles," I said, "Twice each year he emerges from a room full of monitors and screens and sets the clocks in the car and the truck. I have no idea how to change the clocks in the vehicles. I wonder if disconnecting the battery at midnight would reset the clock to 12:00?"

"Wow, I guess that's true. My kids can fix the clocks too. How do they know that?"

"Beats me. It seems like math and English aren't emphasized, so maybe they have clock class or something. They can also get maximum performance from computers and program the television after the power goes out. And yet, placing milk in the refrigerator is way too complicated."

"Maybe they do have a clock class," Lenny said while scratching his chin, "So what are you saying?"

"I am saying that we have to clean our own guns, just as we always should have. And November is the first good month for doing it." I stomped my foot for effect. Lenny walked away talking to himself about car clocks.

But I truly meant what I said. November is great for cleaning guns. Because a certain amount of ambiance is necessary to really enjoy cleaning your guns, and it can't be really found until November. I will detail the steps for you now. A good, enjoyable gun cleaning begins with a good, enjoyable dirtying of said gun. This, of course, is a process that begins early in the morning with solitude. Pre-dawn is when a person, if they are willing, can have a house to himself. November is a little cooler than previous months, and this does wonders to improve the taste of coffee. I have several potlickin' beagles in my house, and they surround me as I sip coffee and look out on the porch for the morning temperature. Frost on the ground is always a nice addition.

By the second cup of coffee I will have made my decision regarding which hound or hounds to take afield. Sometimes this is a deliberate decision based upon some data—experience of the hound, scenting conditions, abundance or scarcity of rabbits. Other times the decision is as arbitrary as determining what dogs are giving me the most eager or pathetic look. I often hunt with two hounds, but have been known to take a whole pack. If I am hunting alone, it can be one dog on many occasions.

The hunt is the most important part of this gun dirtying process. Now there are several ways to dirty a gun. One is to shoot at every rabbit that presents itself, no matter the difficulty of the shot. I haven't done this much since my teenage years, although there have been a couple seasons in recent memory where I have not been able to hunt as much as I would like and so I opted for this perfectly common method of preparing a fine gun for a good cleaning.

Of course, the better way to dirty the gun is to do it with a minimum of shots. I will let the rabbit make at least one full circle before I shoot, and often I will wait for several circles due to the fact that I can find no RDA listing on foodstuffs for a recommended daily allowance of lead. Iron, manganese and other metals are listed, but nothing for lead. I will wait for a clean kill, if I can. A good way to set the groundwork for a gun cleaning is to only really dirty one barrel. I rarely do this.

This brings me to another crucial step in cleaning a shotgun: Clean a nice looking gun. Oh, I know how well a light 12 bore with a synthetic stock (absent of beautiful wood) can swing, and I know how nice it is to have that third shot ready in an autoloader. But a pretty gun is easier to clean. A hinge action is also more convenient for sighting down the bore to ensure final cleanliness. I like a nice 16 gauge myself. Never hesitate to use a good gun. Nothing is so sad as a beautiful double barrel that never leaves the house. It is like a field champion that never runs outside the fence—beautiful, effective, and incredibly underused. I have always admired guys that take their champs to the field. Certainly I am amongst the nameless horde of beaglers never to own a champion, but I have bumped into a few trialers in hunting season, hunting over their champions—it is nice to see.

It is crucial that the gun gets dirty while putting game in the vest, as opposed to getting dirty while missing everything. Sure, who amongst us hasn't flung some no. 71/2 after a grouse that was never in danger of being hit? But make sure that a rabbit or two gets into the vest. It is hard to enjoy cleaning the gun when we shoot poorly. Although, to be fair, I have found that if the beagles are disappointed with a missed shot, it is hard to notice as they continue their joyful, baying, tail-wagging pursuit past the scene of human failure.

Lastly, make sure that you get some debris into the gun. Get some pollen in the rib between the barrels. Goldenrod is great for pushing its way around the safety or trigger guard. A little mud on the butt plate from resting the empty gun against a tree while you retrieve a rabbit is just fine (from the stories I hear from other beaglers, apparently I am the only guy without a beagle that retrieves dead rabbits). After all the shooting, missing, rabbit killing, and brush busting is accomplished, you are ready to take your rabbits home.

Myself, I like to cut the rabbits into pieces and let them soak in saltwater overnight before I do anything more with the meat. After this first task is finished, it is best to eat a good supper. If lucky, there will be rabbit from a previous hunt to cook with cornbread, potatoes, and gravy. If more lucky, a wonderful wife will have this accomplished for you.

The early evening will also include all the drama of the day. Rushing to get things ready for work the next day, catching up with chores around the house, answering the phone calls that come in constantly, returning phone calls that arrived whilst you were hunting and all the rest. Not the least of which is the daily struggle to get a kid or kids to do their homework and brush their teeth and go to bed in some semblance of order. Eventually it will all be done.

Now is the time to clean the gun. Start the kindling in your fireplace and let it get to a nice bed of coals before stoking it with enough wood to shed some light. Cleaning a gun is always more pleasant in front of a roaring fire on bitter evening. There is something about a fire that makes the whole process calming and peaceful. Place all the necessary tools to clean your gun nearby, and make ready a drink to enjoy the process. I like coffee on a cool evening, but if your tastes run towards something cooler, so be it.

No doubt, if your trusty hounds live in the house they will appear at this time. Mine like to lie near my feet or on the back of the couch behind my head. The house is as quiet at this time as it was in the morning. It is peaceful and a gun can be cleaned and wiped and immunized against the elements while listening to the gentle sounds of snoring beagles and a crackling fire. The beagles dream the hunt anew in their snores, paws twitching and mouths chirping quiet sounds of pursuit. I'm remembering the hunt as well, although it seems to me that the dogs must remember it in more detail than I do as they slumber in blissful pursuit. This is what November is for. I clean my own guns, and have no rust on the barrels. Of course November is also the month when we move the clocks backwards, and this will require secret knowledge that is beyond me.

CONTEST

I was down to the local feed store the other day when I happened to run into some beaglers. This is a rare encounter in the feed store, as most of my beagler friends do not make it to the store for one of two reasons—(1) either they stay up all night running dogs and are asleep during business hours, or (2) they refuse to pay money for dog food and instead take it from beagle clubs after trials.

"Hey, Ford!" Dawson Mcaffee called out to me, "I wish you would buy my brand of dog food when you come in here."

"Ah, C'mon now Dawson, you never seem to mind my Purina when you come to take it for your hounds," I answered back, taking a cup of coffee and sitting down to hear the local gab.

"Now Preacher, you know I'm just borrowin' that feed right?" Dawson eyed me in a serious fashion.

"I understand, but remember what I said—borrowed dog food comes back as processed dog food—you can keep that in your kennel!"

The guys around us got a big chuckle out of that. One fellow, who was sitting on the bench across from me, actually spilled his coffee on the porch floor as he shook in mirth.

"Dawson," I said, "Don't you ever buy me any dog food. You're one of the best handymen around, and anytime I know of folks on hard luck you always do house repairs for the cost of materials. You're all right with me. I can live without a few pounds of dog food when you need one night's worth to hold you over till the store opens."

"How's your dogs running?" Shady Burns asked me.

"Not good at all at the moment. It's been so hot that I haven't dared run them in this weather," I answered.

"Why don't you run at night?"

Shady always ran at night and he always insulted everyone's dogs. He called my dogs slowpokes, he called Lenny's hounds mouthy, and he called Daryl's dogs cold-trailers. I guess, in his mind, he had the only dogs worth feeding.

"I dunno. I guess it isn't the same for me. It sounds like rabbit running, but I can't see any dog work. Say, do you boys that run all night chase by miner's light or how do you do that?"

"Shoot!" Shady said, "We just drop the tailgate and sit on it."

"Yeah, I guess that just doesn't seem like fun to me. It won't be long and we'll be through the summer. We can run in the early morning again then," I said, "I gotta get my dogs in shape."

"Your slowpoke hounds can't run with mine at night anyway," Shady bragged. Shady annunciated the words "slow" and "poke" with particular clarity and volume.

"I suspect your right," I said, finishing my coffee, "You have some mighty fast hounds...you just don't know where they are." It felt good to give him an insult back. We all teased each other, but he was mean spirited about it.

"I do too! You come out some night and see." Shady fumed.

"All right then. Let's do this the fair way. Wednesday afternoon we will run dogs for about an hour—no more. It'll be hot. I'll bring a dog and you bring one too. We'll see which is better. Then, Wednesday night we will do the same—and my dog will be faster than yours. But I want to call the places we run," I offered.

"You ain't got a dog faster than my slowest!" Shady bellowed. "You name the place."

Shady couldn't wait to go. We met at the old coal strippings at noon on that Wednesday. I brought my little Rebel, because he has the strongest nose of any dog I own. It wasn't long before we had a large bunny moving and my Rebel and Shady's big male, Gunner, were running.

"My dog jumped that rabbit!" Shady yelled.

"How do you know, were you in the brush?" I asked.

"Nope, but my dog barked first." Shady observed.

"O.K. Sounds good."

The rabbit ran past us and onto the piles of shale and dirt with just a few small patches of scorched vegetation. Both dogs emerged from the briars; Gunner was well in front of my little Rebel. All at once Gunner got quiet. Rebel started to walk, which I might add is embarrassing to watch—but not as embarrassing as watching Gunner. Rebel would bark, walk ahead a few yards, bark again, walk ahead a few more yards and bark again. Every time Rebel would bark, Gunner would jump in front of Rebel and bark once, but would then wander off until Rebel barked again. It took a couple minutes for Rebel to cross the spoil pile but soon he was back in the brush and running again. The pace picked up until the rabbit came back across the dirt and shale again.

Rebel picked his way across the gully one more time, walking slowly and tonguing infrequently. Gunner dove in front of every bawl Rebel emitted, but never could smell the rabbit. You ever see a dog "me-too" from the front? It is possible; I've seen it. Once the chase plunged back into the thickets Gunner would start tonguing again.

The next time the rabbit came out it was the same: Rebel walking and Gunner jumping in front of him. This time Shady jumped in front of Gunner and picked him up. The dogs had not chased long and Rebel was thirsty in that August sun.

"We'll see how your slow-poke dog does tonight!" Shady cried.

"Fine," I said, "I will meet you tonight behind the golf club. How about 9:00?"

"I'll be there."

Shady showed up a few minutes late. "Should be good scent here tonight," I said, and I brought Dawson here to prove which dog is fastest. Now, I want to warn you, that I might calculate speed faster than you. I gauge speed in terms of minutes/circle. You see, I don't care how fast a dog runs, if he takes 5 minutes to solve each check what is the point? Why, I had a dog one time that I couldn't tell if it was solving a check of finding a new rabbit! Sound familiar Shady?"

Shady just glared at me. I continued, "Now Shady, I'm gonna let Rebel out of the car here, and we'll see how many circles he makes in one hour. Then, we will let Gunner out and see how many circles he makes. Sound fair?"

"Ain't they gonna run together?" Shady asked. I knew Gunner was eager, and I also knew that those golf club rabbits ran notoriously long and convoluted circles. They darted across the open areas and made big diameter circles that had lots of checks. I hunt there once the snow is too deep to golf.

"Nah, I wouldn't want to taint the readings any," I said. Rebel jumped out and started a rabbit over by a patch of clover on the edge of the green. "I got a flashlight here, Shady. Let's see if a rabbit comes by here. There are a lot of deer around here too." Sure enough a rabbit squirted past and we started stumbling behind the dog in the dark. Rebel made three circles and then lost the rabbit.

"He only made three circles!" Shady said.

"Yeah, we will have to see what he can do with this last half-hour. That last rabbit either lost the dog or went into a hole. I know a lot of guys that just always seem to know that it went into a hole. But, just for the sake of argument, let's say that the dog lost that one." Within a few minutes Rebel found another rabbit and we verified it with the flashlight. Shady sat on his tailgate, but I followed Rebel through the dark. He ran way faster than I could, but I could cut through some openings and clearings to stay somewhat close.

Rebel was almost through a third circle on that rabbit when Dawson yelled, "TIME! Preacher, I am giving your dog credit for 5 ¾ circles!"

"O.K." I waited for Rebel to come out and I ordered him down and tied him to my tailgate and gave him some water.

Shady ran to his dog and put him down where Rebel was last barking. Gunner took off with enthusiasm. He went into the brush and the rabbit came right back out to us. Within a few minutes the guns of Gunner were silent. I could see a nervous Shady beside me. "Don't worry," I taunted, "He'll catch on here. It's a bit harder when there aren't other dogs solving the checks." Of course, I figured Gunner would be extra quick anyway. The last rabbit scent he had smelled, on the coal spoils, wasn't quite strong enough for him to claim. So he was more than eager on this humid night with a tiny bit of moisture. Gunner never barked again on that rabbit.

"It probably went in a hole and that rabbit we saw was another one," I said.

We heard Gunner again, down over the hill. He barked for a bit, and then fell silent. By the time we got there he was barking further down the hill below us. We went back to where we had parked on the backside of the golf course and soon we heard Gunner tonguing strong. He emerged from the brush on a big deer and screamed over the hill.

"Say Shady, this has been his best performance yet. Since I never stipulated that the dog had to chase a rabbit, do you want us to start timing this circle? Say my dog might be slower than yours, but I know where he is."

"I know where mine is too!" Shady exploded and reached into his pocket. "I have a GPS on him." Sure enough, there it was. It gave a direction and distance and everything. Gunner grew quiet again.

"Say, Shady, how come this thing says that your dog is treeing right now?"

"It is for all kinds of dogs." He fumbled with the buttons.

"I see that," I said, "it says that Gunner is on point now. Well, I was wrong. You certainly do know where your dog is. Just don't let those batteries die." Shady glared at me again.

I never run a good dog—or even a mediocre one like my Rebel—with a dog that can't solo a rabbit. I have always felt that good dogs can learn bad habits, but bad ones never seem to learn good habits. The real shame of it is that Gunner looks good on the ground with a handful of beagles behind him. I'll be out and about with my slowpokes.

THE DIRECTOR OF HOMELAND SECURITY

This is my understanding of the Department of Homeland Security: it is a good thing. It is needed, and does tons of behind-the-scenes work that keeps us safe. At the same time, they issue statements that are highly unusual and can worry people when there is no threat. For instance, when the department was first formed, we were all told to invest in duct tape and plastic. Many since that time have wondered just what Secretary Ridge was thinking. Where did that advice come from? I think the answer is that, as the former governor of Pennsylvania, Ridge simply looked at how many Pennsylvanians winterize their porches with plastic and duct tape! I think the former governor's assumption was that if it can stop winter then it can stop terrorists.

Anyway, the end result is that the Department of Homeland Security can give warnings that are false alarms on occasion but can also monitor the bad guys in a very effective fashion. Better safe than sorry, even if some folks get worked up and worried over nothing once in a while. At my home Zoe is the Director of Homeland Security. A car starts up in my driveway, and she is on the alert. This is very helpful, especially when door-to-door type solicitors are in the neighborhood. Zoe sounds her alarm and the other beagles join the alert. By the time anyone even gets to the porch, a full blast of pack music is slamming through the door.

To further discourage the door-to-door types, I keep my lawn tall and unkempt. How many beaglers do you know with well-manicured lawns? I run dogs early in the morning before work, and sometimes in the evening after work. This summer it seems that any evening I am free it rains—I can run dogs in the rain but I can't mow grass.

The by-product has been that Zoe, and her Department of Homeland Security, in conjunction with a rugged yard, has kept solicitors to an all-time low.

Zoe is the most protective of my hounds. She wants to be by my side at all times. The other hounds would sell me for a cup of dog food. I am little more than the dispenser of *Purina* in their eyes. Zoe is the hound that can truly be called a devoted canine companion (she can run a rabbit too). The other dogs can be very disrespectful of the house. Zoe walks behind them trying to take care of any messes or damage that might upset me. She will not defile the house. I once left her in the house for 16 hours, I was with a family at a hospital and I fully expected to return home to a mess! Zoe, out of desperation, had relieved herself in the bathtub.

She refuses to allow any other hound to receive attention from me either. If another one of my dogs sits on my lap, she will simply lay on top of that dog until it can't breathe. When it gets up for air, she takes post on my lap.

The drawback of my Director of Homeland Security is that she will sometimes bark out false alarms. I have awoken from a dead sleep to run into the living room and find Zoe barking at nothing. It took me months to realize that she was barking at the furnace when it first starts with a "WHOOSH!".

It isn't uncommon for Zoe to upgrade a threat level to orange alert when the refrigerator compressor starts running. And I have seen Zoe go straight to red alert as she sits from her post on the back of the sofa and barks at her own reflection moving in the picture window across the room in the late evening. The spin cycle of the washing machine can also be perceived as danger, and this results in her leading her pack-mates downstairs to the basement to let the washing machine know where it stands in the cosmic pecking order that has been worked out in Zoe's little canine brain.

A while back a parishioner stopped by the house to drop off some paperwork for a committee meeting. He was greeted by the standard chorus of alarm that was initiated by the Director of Homeland Security. He came into the house expecting a viscous onslaught of dogteeth, but instead discovered a greeting of flicking tongues and excited whimpers from the hounds. All of them greeted the stranger with open mouths wanting a snack. All but Zoe, who sniffed him over, waited for me to sit, and then jumped up on my lap. She isn't mean, but she is loyal.

The neighbors have a yap dog that basically barks off and on throughout the day. It is one of those little tiny dogs with hair that drips to the ground, and has a bark that, through selective breeding, has been designed to imitate the sound of fingernails on chalkboards. This little rat dog is Zoe's nemesis. She wages a daily war of words with this dog. I can only imagine what is being said.

"I hate your bark you ratty little mutt!"

"I lived in this neighborhood first you ugly beagle!"

"Who you calling ugly, rat!"

"You're ugly!"

"If I could get through this fence, I would show you something!"

"Just be glad that I am on this stake or *you* would be sorry!"

Of course to the rest of the county the whole thing sounds very much like barking dogs. And a lot of barking at that. This is especially true if Zoe can enlist some help from my other dogs

"Hey Shadow, tell that mutt that he can't cause any grief around here!"

"Yeah, just what Zoe said, you moron!" Shadow resounds.

"Hey, what is going on over here!" another beagle chimes.

Before you know it the rat dog either shuts up, or its owner walks out and takes him back inside in the face of the wall of pack music bellowing through the hills. Zoe walks confidently back into the house and takes up her post on the back of the sofa. From there she awaits the next threat to my safety. It might be the TV. Maybe the microwave will make a beep. Whatever the threat might be I will surely know. In fact she is barking right now. Let me go see what the commotion seems to be about...I think that there are a couple of guys in suits walking up towards the house in the fenced lawn. It's hard to tell though because the grass is high. It looks like we have gone to condition yellow in the house for the moment. And if these guys stopped at the neighbors and pet that rat dog and Zoe catches any of its odor; we will be at red in a hurry. Eternal vigilance is the price of freedom. And also whatever money it takes to buy duct tape and plastic for your porch.

DEEP-FRIED HI-TECH BEAGLING

It was not quite dark when the phone rang. I was reading, and not willing to answer, "Can somebody get that?" I yelled, hoping that it might be my neighbor, Ronald. He never seems to be home when I want to visit him. You see, he has one of those super-duper satellite packages with all the sporting events you could ever want to watch. I had been leaving messages for him to record some things for me, but he hasn't called me back. My cable can't get all the Penguin hockey matches.

"It's your loser friend," my wife replied, looking at the Caller I.D. function, the phone still ringing. Whatever else we can say about technology, it does allow us to see who is calling.

"Which of my friends is the loser?" I asked.

"Which one is not?"

The phone quit ringing.

"Great!" I grumbled, "Now the phone's stopped. It could have been an emergency or sporting news."

"I'm sure it was an emergency—a dog probably ate something, or a junk 4x4 broke down, or somebody placed 2nd at a trial and not 1st and it is the end of the world, or...."

"Could you please tell me who called? If it was a loser, in your opinion, then I am guessing it was Jimbo."

"Nope, Lenny."

I called Lenny, and it was busy. Then I tried again and again. "I can't get through!" I panicked.

"That's because you morons are both trying to call each other at once." My wife proffered, "Just sit back and let the phone ring."

I hung up the phone and waited. Nothing happened. I called Lenny.

"Hello?" he answered.

"What happened?" I asked.

"My wife says that we were both calling each other at once."

"Mine says that too. She told me to hang up and wait for you to call." I said.

"Yeah, my wife said that too and then no one called."

"Yeah, I waited for like 10 minutes too."

"You both stopped calling each other at the same time!" Lenny's wife screamed loud enough to be heard through the phone.

"I hate new technology," I said.

"Me too," Lenny countered, "Wanna go with me to get a machine that converts cook oil into diesel? I gotta get the contraption and 220 gallons of used cooking grease."

"Yeah, I'll go, what could go wrong?" I hung up the phone.

My wife called to me as I grabbed my coat, "Was it an emergency?"

"Nope, it was the solution to an emergency."

Now, in case you are wondering, here is the nature of the emergency. Lenny and I have a spot close to home that is perfect for rabbits. We don't hunt there, except maybe once a season to thin out the rabbit population a little bit. A neighboring beagler found the spot last summer when he was visiting relatives and heard our dogs chasing. He returned to that location throughout the rabbit season and has virtually exterminated the population there. It will take a year or two, at least, to recover a good training grounds population. What few rabbits are left always go underground very early in a chase.

So, our new spot is quite some distance from home. As you may have noticed, fuel costs are up. Lenny is a pretty good mechanic and he put a diesel engine in his truck and bought the parts necessary to run the thing on cook oil. He has also secured the exclusive rights to the used cook oil in about a dozen local businesses. Now, you may ask, how Lenny could get that many places to give him used oil, given the demand for such things these days. The short answer is that they are all bars and Lenny is in dart, pool, and other leagues that frequent every one of those establishments. He basically threatened to withhold his business from any bar that would not donate. It is kind of a grease-based extortion. Lenny and his compatriots have kept many bars in the profit margins over the years.

The last component that Lenny needed was a conglomeration of filters that somehow allows you to dump the grease in one end and have it emerge from the other side as automotive grade diesel. I was on the porch when Lenny pulled in with his truck.

"Free fuel, here we come!"

"Where did you find this filter that we're going to pick up?"

"Some college kid built it. He's a graduate student, an engineer of some kind. He's getting rid of his car."

"Well, wait a minute. Are you sure that the thing works if his own car is broke?"

"His motor is fine. It's an old VW. But the transmission is shot and the tie-rod ends and steering linkage are worthless and the body is rotted away by salt. The damn motor outlived its body. I'm gonna pay the kid 300 bucks for the filter and the oil he has stored up."

"300 bucks won't fix his car or get him a new one!" I said.

"No, but it is what the engineer needs to go to Spring Break with his friends."

"You're a crook!"

"Thanks."

We arrived at a section of student slums—off campus housing with landlords who do no maintenance on the buildings and subdivide each structure so as to maximize the number of students who can live in each home. The houses are closely packed with small yards consisting mostly of garbage and beer cans. Lenny parked next to a failing VW Jetta and began loading a contraption that can best be described as a bunch of plastic buckets with hoses. I then helped him load four 55 gallon drums that required us to back the truck up to a porch and roll the barrels from that porch onto the tailgate and into the bed of the truck. A skinny fellow with a laptop emerged and Lenny gave him a wad of cash. The guy counted the money, clicked a key on his computer and rejoiced over the fact that he just reserved his ticket to the collegiate hedonism that is Spring Break.

We sped off to Lenny's garage. After unloading all the barrels and filters, I went home. I would have stayed to help Lenny convert the motor to bio-diesel, but it is generally agreed that I cause more problems in the garage than I solve. In fact, Lenny has not allowed me to help him in the garage since I hooked up the plugs of his Ford to the distributor following the numbering scheme for a Chevy. I assured him that I had followed the right pattern, not knowing that Ford and Chevy numbered the pistons of a V-8 in a different way. It took him two days to find my mistake. I went home while Lenny tinkered on the engine.

Several days later Lenny showed up at the house in his truck. It sounded the same, but there was an odd odor. It seemed to smell like...French fries. "What is that smell? Can't you smell that smell?" I asked, quoting a Lynyrd Skynyrd song.

"It's my exhaust."

"Can you smell it in the cab?"

"Sometimes, but only if you are idling with the window down," he said, turning off the engine. We walked into the kitchen of my house.

My wife walked into the house, "What are you guys cooking in here?"

"Nothing," I answered.

She looked in the microwave. It was clean. "I guess you guys aren't cooking. Nothing blew up in there and I don't think either one of you can use a kitchen stove."

"I can make sandwiches," Lenny said, "If you're hungry. But we don't usually like the bread that you buy—it tastes like bird seed."

"I'm not hungry, but I smell...deep fried fish or something." My wife said.

"Oh, that's just my work coat, it took a while to fine tune my engine when I converted it to run on grease." Lenny explained.

Renee quickly left the kitchen muttering something about not wanting to know anything about grease and something else about the fact that only bird-brains would actually know what bird seed tasted like.

"Let's run dogs!" Lenny said. And we did. To be honest, we have run dogs every day since then. Lenny has gallons and gallons of fuel. It is amazing no-cost beagling. To be fair, I have paid for all the coffee and snacks on our commutes, because Lenny paid for all the equipment. There is just this one problem. You know that Pavlov guy who could condition dogs to salivate to a bell by feeding them when he rang the bell? Well, my beagles are conditioned to go nuts over certain stimuli as well. For instance, if I ring one of the bells that I put on their collars when we chase rabbits, they get excited. If they see me grab my brush pants or a shotgun or a leash they will likewise erupt in anticipation. When I drive to running grounds they will start barking when I leave the hardtop and hit the dirt roads.

After running rabbits every day with Lenny, and getting to the grounds in his new bio-diesel truck, the dogs now get very excited whenever they smell any fried foods. My wife fries very little food, so this hasn't been much of a problem. But it has been the Lenten season, and one of the local Roman Catholic priests likes the outdoors—he has bird dogs. He stopped by the house after his church's weekly Friday fish fry fund-raiser. He walked into the yard where the dogs were, and they went absolutely bonkers. He was covered in mud and dog hair. To think, that among other things, the high cost of fuel has set the ecumenical movement back in my community. I tried to tell the good Father that the whole affair was easily explained if one were familiar with Pavlov and his experiments. He should feel lucky, my neighbor Ronald is a manager at a fast-food restaurant and when the wind is blowing the dogs always know when he gets home. I can find him when he sneaks home now, and I should see all the Penguin matches for the remainder of the season.

BUILDING A BETTER DOG BOX

My father could build things. Anything. If it was made out of wood, he could make it. He passed away, but I own some of the tools that he had accumulated over a lifetime of building things. Dad supplemented his paycheck from the factory by doing remodeling jobs: roofs, bathrooms, kitchens, porches, garages, whatever. He would even take his vacation to work jobs that paid better than his employer. I often got to help dad on these ventures. It was my job to measure things improperly, bend nails, step on nails, spill things, and lose important items. Those were all things that I did well.

Dad was even my best physician when it came to recovering from work-related injuries. You see, I always managed to get hurt on weekends. Weekends are when real doctors leave the ER and the incoming, not yet ripe crop of doctors, fill in. These are the young bucks and does who aren't quite ready to be in their own practice. It is a lot like having a substitute teacher in the classroom, "My note says to tell you to finish your homework and sit quietly," the doctor said.

"Thanks Doc, but I am bleeding here, did you notice?"

"That isn't on my list, why don't we just hold on 'til my supervisor gets back?" The intern replied.

"When will that be?"

"Monday morning."

"It's Saturday now. I might run out of blood by then."

"We could start an I.V.," he said without confidence as he looked around over his shoulder, "NURSE! OVER HERE PLEASE!"

On one such construction accident, I managed to find an antique nail—the square kind and embed like a CNN reporter into the sole of my foot for safekeeping. The on-call student gave me a tetanus shot and sent me home. I awoke to find a red line of blood poisoning snaking its way from my foot and setting up a siege just south of my body parts necessary for reproduction. Dad drove me back to the student at the ER. I was on the cusp of puberty at the time and was having fears of such things as amputation and other nasty treatments if the blood poisoning continued on its path north. I was given antibiotics and sent home. The red army retreated and vanished, but my foot ached until dad took a hot knife and removed a piece of my boot sole from my foot, something that the ER doctors missed twice.

Anyway, after dad passed away, I inherited a lot of things that I knew how to use—rifles, shotguns, and fishing poles. I also inherited things that I couldn't use: construction tools. I know how to use tools; I just can't seem to make my hands do what my eyes have seen others do. When it comes to carpentry skills, this apple landed close to the tree, but then rolled down hill some distance before coming to a rest. The thing is though, that when you have tools, you feel compelled to use them. The tools call to you and make you believe that they will be obedient in your hands. This happened to me once while I was looking at the top-of-the-line dog boxes advertised in dog supply catalogs. The tools kept calling and they decided that I could maybe build a better dog box.

I wanted to build it for in the back of my toy. By toy I mean a 1978 FJ-40 with a Chevy engine under the hood..."If your pastor drives a Land Cruiser with a 4 inch lift kit, 35 inch tires, and a small-block 400, you might be a redneck..."

Looking through the catalogs I discovered that I could not buy a box to use all of the space in the back of my buggy. I would have been forced to buy a two-dog box for a compact truck. A four-dog box wouldn't fit between the rear fender wells. And those high quality boxes are quite expensive. Building my own would save money. My plan was to build a box that would use all of the space in the rear cargo area—stretch it out over the fender wells to get the width necessary for 4 separate compartments, and then put storage areas underneath to prevent the box from sagging. I like storage compartments. I started measuring and drawing. Measuring and drawing is the fun and easy part of the job.

The idea was to make the box in pieces and then assemble it inside the vehicle. The components would consist of a floor, 4 walls, three dividers, and roof. I then bought the lumber and started building. I spared no expense in the construction process. I sometimes cut two or even three versions of each part to be sure that it was satisfactory. My wife claimed that such extra components were due to craftsman error, and that I should not have needed to build 13 walls in order to get 4 that I liked. I explained to her the nature of templates and precision.

Another complication was that I built this dog box in the winter. My garage is not insulated or heated, so this meant that I had to do all of the work in the basement. The basement is also the laundry room. Nothing endears you to your spouse quite like having her wade through six inches of sawdust to carry a basket of clothes to the washing machine. I also learned that wood glue doesn't wash out of a dress very easy, did you know that? My wife let me know this.

You haven't lived until you use a lint brush to remove sawdust from your clothes on a daily basis. Forced air heat also allowed us to enjoy the smell of milled lumber throughout the entire house. I never knew my wife was allergic to wood dust before. I think she is grateful that I helped her learn that without having to go to an allergy specialist and get pricked with needles. I could tell that she was thankful by the way she seemed to pray more during the 9 weeks that it took me to build the dog box. "Thank you Lord for my husband," and "Give me strength, God, give me strength," were things that she would say during the construction process. You need strength when you have allergies.

I wanted the box to look presentable. I also thought that it would be nice if I could reach behind me and maybe pat a dog on the head. So I made that back wall out of vertical dowels. There is just something about cylindrical wood that has "Class" written all over it. The doors were wooden framed with galvanized wire covering the frame. I used brass hinges, of course. I even put some cedar on the floor inside. It was leftover from a closet project that my neighbor was doing. It was actually hard to get that cedar. I would stop over with my tools to help whenever I heard Fred working on the closet, but he must have been quite busy since he never answered the door when I knocked. He had himself locked in too. Funny thing is that a few times I thought that I saw him looking out the window towards my house. Anyway, I came home from church one day and found the cedar on the porch. Fred must have gotten my messages.

When it came time to install the box in the vehicle I couldn't have been more excited. I was even more excited when I realized that I would have the unexpected joy of taking the roof off my buggy to get the box installed. Taking the roof off my Land Cruiser was no trouble. It required a 10 mm socket and 4 men and a boy to lift it. Several hours, many bruises, and 6 pizzas (had to pay the 4 men and the boy. That kid ate a lot of pizza!) later, it was all in one piece and ready to haul dogs. I decided to take the dogs to the beagle club.

Upon arriving, I put two dogs on the ground and left two in the box. I heard a commotion coming from the vehicle and walked over to see that my biggest male, Shadow, had broken through the wall with the vertical dowels. He did this partially by chewing and partially by plowing through the wall because he wanted to run rabbits. Looking at the size of the hole that he made, I could see that I would have no trouble reaching behind me to pat him on the head.

On the way home Shadow sat in the passenger seat. He had customized his box to the point that he could walk in and out with ease. He would sit on the seat for a while and then walk back into his compartment to smell the other dogs. I wondered what could be done to fix the problem. I finally decided that I would have to start all over and make a stronger box. No soft-pine dowels this time. I would have to make dowels from hardwood. This would mean borrowing a wood lathe....

As I began the task of rebuilding, I noticed a catalog with the expensive dog boxes. I looked at what I spent on supplies. Hmmmmm. Those boxes aren't really that expensive, especially when you factor in your time. I have to put dad's tools up. He would have been proud of me, I'm sure. I didn't step on any nails or trip even once. I never even cut myself... Well, maybe my pride was hurt a little when the girl at the drive-thru laughed at me for trying to hold Shadow from jumping out of the window, "Mister, why don't you just put that dog inside that crate you have there? It would make it easier for you to eat."

"Yeah, it would be easier, but then I couldn't pat him on the head while I drove."

THE FARM

Dod and Marge Macentyre live on a small "farm" outside of town. They moved there from the city and they are real nice people. I remember the first time I went to their farm; I was invited for a Christmas party. Dod is my dentist, and although his family isn't real big on religion, they did ask me out to the farm to say a prayer before the meal. I was most impressed by the large sign on the lane up to the farm that read, "Macentyre Farm." I had an opportunity to talk with Marge and Dod during a time period of mingling

"Plant much corn in the spring?" I asked.

"Huh?" Marge answered.

"The farm. Do you plant corn?"

"No," Dod answered, "We aren't growing corn."

"Beans?"

"No," Dod answered, "No beans either."

"How many heads are you milking?"

Dod and Marge looked at me with blank stares.

"Beefers?" I asked.

They responded with more confusion. Marge scratched her head. Dod looked as if I might be speaking a language besides English. Finally, Dod spoke, "What are you talking about?"

"Just what do you raise on this farm?"

"We grow pussy willow bushes," Marge chimed in and Dod chimed out. Marge continued, "We don't believe in making animals work, so we do not keep any livestock on the farm." Dod was slinking into his chair as Marge geared up for her promotional ad for the farm, "I also grow a very large garden during the summer because I am a vegetarian, but pussy willow bushes and flowers comprise the bulk of the farms crops. And some fruit trees."

"Do you allow hunting on your farm?" I asked.

Marge shook visibly, dropped her glass of imported water, and streaked up the stairs crying. I feared that perhaps she was having a seizure. Dod explained to me that Marge was terribly opposed to hunting and could not bear the thought of an animal being eaten, not even by other animals. He also explained that he would often sneak out of the house to have a carnivorous meal on occasion. I saw Dod several times after that. He would stop by the house for a burger, or something like that, but I did not see Marge again until this past summer.

Marge and Dod showed up on the porch. My wife let them in. I was placing burnt burger that sat too long from the new grill in the dogs' food bowl.

"How's the pussy willow farm?" I asked

Marge was all business, "Mr. Ford, I understand that you own highly trained canines that live for killing rabbits?" Marge had a crazed look in her eye, the kind of look that Hollywood bad-guys take years to perfect. It was the look of someone who had undergone some serious psychological trauma.

"Well," I replied, "That depends on how loosely you use the term 'highly-trained'."

"What I mean," Marge growled through clenched teeth, "Is will they kill my rabbits?"

"Uh, what was that Marge?" I was caught off guard by her words, as she seemed so opposed to hunting the last time I saw her.

"The rabbits. I want them all gone from my farm. Every last one."

"Marge, I think maybe you should calm down, maybe you're spending too much time with the pussy willows," I said.

At that she burst into tears. Dod put his arm around Marge to console her and then he offered me an explanation, "The rabbits ate away the bark on her pussy willows. They're in poor shape. Same thing happened to her apple trees and plum trees."

"I'm real sorry to hear that Dod, is she O.K.?"

"M-m-m-my," Marge stammered through tears, "My lettuce is gone too, and my ra-ra-ra-radishes." Her eyes turned to narrow slits that could burn a hole through lead,

"Where are these beagles, Mr. Ford? I want every last one of those rodents removed from my farm. And I want you and your dogs to make that happen!"

We walked down to the basement where the dogs were lying on the cool cement to avoid the summer heat. "Here they are," I flourished, "My highly trained hounds." Shadow and Rebel were laying side-by-side on the floor. One of them, probably Shadow, let out a noxious odor that hung thick in the air. Rebel yawned himself awake and walked out into the yard where he promptly flopped into a pile of goop and rolled in it.

"They do not seem very ferocious, Mr. Ford," Marge commented. Shadow jumped onto Dod's lap and Rebel wandered back into the house to get his belly rubbed. Rebel's breath smelled like a dumpster. Shadow placed his head against Dod's head and let out a belch. He is so affectionate that way.

"No ma'am, they are not ferocious at all. Oh, don't get me wrong, if you were to drop a scrap of table food between them right now you would see some excitement, but nothing dangerous or injuring."

"These pooches will take care of my rabbit problem?" Marge asked with a doubtful look on her face.

"Well, they will certainly chase the rabbits. I will have to do my job in harvesting the game as it presents itself."

"Harvest?" Marge thundered through those clenched teeth of hers, "I want these rabbits killed."

At this moment my wife entered the conversation, "Call it harvest, call it kill, reality is my husband doesn't take his limit most of the time."

"I am conserving wildlife," I defended myself.

"Well, you seem to use a lot of ammunition in your conservation endeavors."

I decided to change the topic, "I certainly enjoy hunting Marge, but I only shoot what I can eat." I glanced over and saw that Dod was blue in the face, "Shadow, get off of Dod." Shadow slinked off to the floor, and Dod let out a gasp of air in relief. "Sometimes he gets gas," I explained, "Especially after he eats burnt food. I am still getting the hang of this gas barbeque grill. Just tell that dog to leave when he gets too much to be around. Anyway, Marge, like I was saying I will not shoot a rabbit just to shoot it. There are ethics that must be followed, and I will not waste rabbit meat and I will not disrespect the game or the land."

Dod had his breath back by now, "So what you are saying, Rev. Ford, is that you would need more people eating this rabbit meat before you would shoot more rabbits?"

"Correct, but even so, I would not shoot all of your rabbits. It would be irresponsible."

"Not to mention impossible with his shooting abilities," My wife added.

"Say," Dodd began with a look of glee in his eyes, "What if Marge and I started eating rabbit meat?"

"Great idea," I replied, "I could hold rabbit dinners here at the house and you guys could come over. I could fire up the barbeque grill."

Shadow leaped up from the prone position and got excited at the mention of the word grill. He ran into the kitchen and ate the burnt burger in the food bowl and then returned looking for Dod's lap. Dod was still standing. When he walked my way, I stood up, "Excuse me," I said, "While I let these dogs outside for awhile."

"Do you guys like rabbit meat?" I asked.

"I do," Dod answered, "Marge does not eat meat."

"I am willing to try," Marge said.

"Well, I will nuke some rabbit in the microwave and thaw it out and then cook it on the grill for us," I said grabbing my spatula and heading for the yard. The dogs were already at the grill, looking on with anticipation.

"How about if I cook the rabbit, dear," My wife intercepted, "Maybe they aren't ready for your gourmet carboned rabbit."

"Sure I responded and I will take Dod and Marge out to see the hounds run some rabbits."

At that we went to the farm where I let the dogs run. Marge almost seemed to enjoy herself. She was especially fond of the beagles and the way that they ran, although she was somewhat distracting when she yelled threats of doom at the rabbits as they streaked past. Her threats scared the rabbits a great deal. I would be glad to recommend Marge to anyone who is looking to test a dog for gun-shyness. You really haven't had the full beagling experience until you have seen someone from Manhattan wearing designer clothes and shouting threats at an innocent rabbit. Shadow and Rebel came through after the rabbit. Marge encouraged them, "Avenge my pussy willows!

After awhile, we returned to the house, where my wife had prepared a delicious rabbit supper from rabbits harvested last year. She did not utilize the grill, but had managed to prepare a lovely meal using the microwave and stove top. It was delicious. Marge did not eat any of the meat as she had thought she might, but she was quite pleased to see that everyone else was eating some. After the meal the Macentyres left.

"Thanks for supper, Bob," Dod said with a satisfied rub of the belly.

"Yes, thank you," Marge seconded, "And feel free to chase those rabbits on the farm anytime, and make sure you hunt there this fall. If you will excuse me, I must sit down from all of this outdoor activity." She kissed Dod and explained that she would meet him in the car.

"Dod," I began, "I am serious about not over-hunting your land. I will shoot some, but...."

"Don't worry," Dod interrupted, "You do what is best for the rabbits and for the dogs. Invite me to a few meals and we will let Marge think as she will about hunting. I, for one, know that hunters are among the best conservationists around."

"Thanks, Dod, and we will take a few rabbits here and there for eating." A loud honking sound came from the driveway as Marge was impatient. Dod and I shook hands.

I have run rabbits at the farm about once a week since that summer meal. It will be a great hunting spot this year. Marge always peeks out her window with satisfaction every time the hounds go by. It is such a nice running ground that I may even make some wire guards for her bushes and trees to protect them this winter. I think Marge might appreciate that. But that might make her no longer need me or my highly-trained hounds. Speaking of the hounds, Shadow must be eating off the grill again. Pew! "Go outside boy!"

RABBIT HUNTING FASHION

My wife was watching television while I was talking on the phone. One of the problems in this scenario is that I am almost unable to speak softly. This is because I have a hunter's ear, which means a little damaged. As my wife says, "Bob has the hearing of a man who has killed a thousand rabbits and missed twice as many grouse."

"You are talking too loud, I can't hear the T.V."

"Sorry, I'll go in the other room."

"Your still too loud, honey. Try going outside!" She called from the living room.

I finished my phone call and returned. "What is so important about this show anyway?" I asked.

"Shh. This woman is getting new clothes," My wife shushed me without removing her gaze from the television. I finished watching the program with her.

"There, how was that?" She beamed, "Isn't it much better than the Discovery Channel or History Channel shows that you watch? That woman just got $5,000 dollars in new clothes to change her look. Wasn't that great?" My wife glowed at the idea of that much clothing.

"Nah. That was a twiggy woman trying to tell another woman what to wear."

"Yeah, but there was a guy helping her out too."

"True, but I got the impression that he didn't really like women all that much. I guess that might be an asset for the fashion industry, who knows. I never understood fashion. Just wear clothes that fit and suit the weather, what else need you worry about?" I grumbled.

"You have definite fashion rules that you follow, so don't give me that!"

"Like what?" I protested.

"Like your ball caps. You change hats every time you get into and out of the car in hunting season. It's like watching Mr. Rogers change his shoes every time he leaves the house or goes in. What's up with that?"

"Orange. I hate orange. I only wear it in the field when the law requires it but that isn't fashion."

"Yes it is. Think about it," and with a smug movement of her hair, she left the room. So I did think about it, and I do have some rules for hunting and clothing. I thought I would share them with you, and perhaps you will agree with me on a few.

No ORANGE, PLEASE

Why bother training your hounds and conditioning them for the hunt if you are going to advertise your hunting spots. All that does is tell the lazy hunter where the rabbits are. I get so tired of the guys who tie a beagle on a chain for 9 months each year and wonder why the hound can't perform well for the 9 days over 3 months that he hunts. I never wear my hunting vest in the car and I never wear an orange hat. I drive in a way that you might think I'm going to the grocery store. I work too hard to find rabbits to throw it away by helping Elmer Fudd.

No NEW CLOTHES

There is nothing so bad as walking into the woods with brush pants that still have the shiny factory coating on them. It is embarrassing really. It puts you in the same class as the city-slickers who clog up Wal-Mart on the day before deer season to buy ammunition, gloves, hats or even a gun. Have some class and get all that stuff early, so that when you enter the field you look like a beagler—smelly, muddy, and briar-torn. The best way to achieve this is to never buy hunting clothes at Wal-Mart. I am a big fan of *Filson* hunting clothes. Yeah, they are expensive, but you only buy them once; Wal-Mart hunting vests will last me a week. My *Filson* is so old I wouldn't be surprised if it is no longer made and a newer version has replaced it. By the way, if the *Filson* folks are reading this, I regularly brag about your products. You could send me a little gift. A pair of boots would be just fine (size 11 wide).

Go EASY ON THE CAMOUFLAGE

I like camo for archery season and turkey hunting. But there is no need to enter the woods looking like mercenaries to hunt rabbits. On the way home from a rabbit hunt, we decided to stop in a restaurant and get a meal. There was a fellow in there dressed in his best tree patterned camo with face paint and one of those sniper-type nettings that look like a pile of leaves on his back. I am not sure what he was hunting, but there is no need to go to such extremes, especially for small game. Oh, the funniest part was that he had a fluorescent orange vest over the whole assembly. It just seems strange to see someone cramming food through a painted face and wearing an orange vest. Maybe I am wrong here, but what is next, your favorite shotgun on the table while you eat?

A POCKETKNIFE WILL DO

I carry a pocketknife for field dressing everything from small game to deer. There is no need to strap a Rambo survival knife on while you are looking for a 2-pound rabbit. Do we really need to carry a whetstone with a great big Viking-style sword into the woods with us? Will you really dull the knife getting the hide off a rabbit? This knight-in shining-armor approach to knives seems odd, especially at the restaurant with the face paint to go with it. Might I recommend a nice Case pocketknife made with care in Bradford, PA. Oh, if the folks at Case are reading, I also recommend your products with some frequency and could use a new knife.

I don't know that these are fashion guidelines, as my wife suggests, but I like to think that it might be classified as some good common sense. Maybe I will see you in the restaurant over a bowl of soup as we tell stories about the day's hunt. You can find me on the other side of the restaurant and I won't be wearing any face paint or Conan the Barbarian's sword. I will probably have a little camo on my ball cap hat. The orange will be in the car. I might be talking a little too loud, but I have decided to preserve what is left of my hearing by using those contraptions that let you hear but quiet muzzle blast. Happy Hunting.

Firewood

A great deal of my youth was dedicated to wood, more specifically, firewood. My father's views and philosophy on fatherhood would prevent him from being a parent today. One of the central pillars of his parenting beliefs was chores. Chores started from a very early age and increased in frequency and difficulty with each birthday. I remember being a "helper" in grade school for my dad on various carpentry jobs that he did in the summer when he took his vacations from the factory. I swept sawdust, cleaned tools, and carried things to and fro. As I got older, I had more and more duties but by the time I was a teenager my life seemed to be completely consumed by one chore: get enough firewood for the winter.

Such parenting would not be tolerated today. We live in an age where kids do not play outside, much less work there. I know my sister's kids get an allowance for picking up their toys. My "allowance" was primarily in the form of my father allowing me to get my own job if I wanted to have cash. My dad was a child in the depression era and was the same age as my friends' grandfathers. There were many ways that I had more in common with my peers' parents than with my peers. Anyway, heating costs were a driving concern for those of us who heated with natural gas during the 1980's and many working families changed back to either wood or coal heat. I only occasionally drive past the house I was raised in and every time I go by, I am utterly amazed that there is no wood stacked in the yard. Like I said, wood dominated my time.

Have you ever counted the number of times that a piece of wood is handled before it is burned for heat? I have. First, you cut the wood down in the forest. Secondly, you cut the wood into manageable chunks. In the third handling, you load those chunks into the truck. The fourth touch involves unloading that wood into the yard. Fifthly, you split that wood. The sixth step is when you stack that split wood in the yard and cover it with a tarp. The seventh phase of this process requires that you take that split wood to the basement. Eighth, you stack that wood again in the basement. The ninth, and last time you touch the wood, is to place it into the furnace. I ought to know.

I still remember how happy I was to get my driver's license, and then how much work it meant when I realized that I could now drive out to the woods alone and get fuel. Dad and I would cut cords of wood and leave it on the ground and then I would be responsible for going back and loading it into the truck and bringing it home.

I learned a lot from doing that work. I learned that I would rather cut and drag ash trees three hundred yards out of the woods as opposed to cutting most maples lying next to the road. All you need to do is split wood and you will see why. I went out of my way to get the easy splitting ash. One of my fondest memories revolves around firewood. During the summer months, while gathering wood for the winter I happened upon a special spot that was just full of grouse and rabbit. In fact, the area was almost overrun with game.

When fall came around, I remembered that spot and I was getting ready for school one morning when I hatched a plan. I went into the yard to water the dogs as I did every morning. Dad had left for work and mom had left to take my aunt to a hospital visit at the "heart specialist." I put my two beagles, Duke and Princess, into the truck and placed my hunting gear into the cab. I drove to school and left the hounds in their dog boxes and all my hunting gear in the truck. I shudder now to think of the ramifications of a boy leaving hunting gear—including a shotgun—in the truck near school grounds today. I locked up the old F-250's doors and I locked the bed cap too. I went to school long enough to be counted as present for homeroom. When the bell rang for first period I went into the hallway and out a side door and into the brush. I walked through thick vegetation for some distance and emerged where I had parked. Time to hunt.

That old F-250 bounced down the rutted logging road with reckless abandon. I couldn't wait to get to the woods. The morning was just perfect. "Hunt 'em up!" I encouraged the dogs as they leaped off the tailgate.

Princess was barking before she had even landed and Duke was harking in before he could even hike a leg to a tree. I shot the first two rabbits by 10:00. That was pretty good considering the fact that I didn't get to the spot until 9:15. By 10:30 I had missed a dozen grouse and was seriously starting to wonder if I would run out of ammunition. It seemed that every time the dogs came by, a grouse or two or three flushed.

I had a 20 gauge, bolt action, Western Auto brand Shotgun. I bought it for 60 bucks with paper route tips when I was twelve, and as far as I was concerned it was the best gun ever made. It had a clip that held two rounds and one in the action. I was making a regular habit of missing a grouse and then seeing the rabbit blur by as I tried to work the bolt to lay a bead on him, only to have another bird flush. It was all the fun a seventeen-year-old boy could want without a girlfriend.

I ate lunch at 11:00. It was a bit early but I needed to return to the truck to look for some ammo. Scattered in the glove box was some old 20 gauge ammo. It was the kind with the paper casing and I wasn't sure how long it had been in the truck, but it was all that was left.

Duke and Princess were five-years-old and really in their prime. By noon I had managed to take my third and fourth rabbits. That was my limit for bunnies and then I was able to waste the rest of my shells on the elusive ruffed grouse. I had a handful of paper cased shells left.

There was the repeated pattern of *whirr* from the wings, *boom* from the gun, and more *whirr* from the wings as the grouse flew off unharmed. I know now, looking back, that I was shooting well beyond the range of that gun and at shots that were very difficult into the saplings. The pattern continued: *whirr, boom, whirr.* But, on the second to the last shot, I managed to down a grouse. I was thrilled. Walking to the truck I had just one round left when something caught my attention from the corner of my eye. I will confess today that I felt no shame then as I blasted that sitting grouse off the branch that he was perched upon! I bagged a second bird after missing so many.

At about that time it began to rain a downpour of the biggest, coldest, November drops of rain I ever felt. At this juncture of the story, it is worth noting that Dad's F-250 was two wheel drive. Now, I am a dyed-in-the-wool Chevy man but that bias has nothing to do with the statement that I am about to make: A two wheel drive Ford pickup can't get out of its own way, let alone take you anywhere in the mud, the snow, or even on wet pavement. In the event that a representative of the Ford motor company is reading this column, I will only retract that statement if I, Bob Ford, am recognized as a long lost relative with all the rights and privileges that go with that status. In that case, then I would be willing to blame what happened next strictly upon the foreboding conditions and torrential rain.

I can't count the number of times I got stuck on the way out of the woods that day. I would get stuck, rock my way out, go forward a few yards and get stuck again. Eventually, I was unable to go at all. The tires were loaded full with clay-laden mud. I sat there in the cab of Dad's truck wondering how I would get home before three o'clock when my father returned from work. I was just starting to be sorry that I ever cut firewood at that place and discover the great hunting when it hit me- firewood!

I leaped out of the cab and began searching for some wood. I loaded up the bed with whatever wood I could find. Most of it was knotty, twisted maple that would make me pay the price for this hooky-hunt through many hours of splitting. Lugging the knotty wood in that blowing storm tore half my shirt and muddied the other half but the plan worked. I had just enough grip from the added weight to slip and slide out to the hardtop. I was as pleased as I could be.

Dad and I arrived home simultaneously. I got ready to face the music. Dad looked at the truck and all of the mud that hung around it and then he looked at my soggy, sorry self. He laughed out loud, and I smiled.

"How many times did you miss?" Dad asked.

"Why?"

"Because, your shirt is ripped and you either got gangrene in that right shoulder, or one hell of a black, blue and green mark is starting to form from so much shootin'."

I never did get in trouble for that day. Dad didn't care, it seemed. He wanted me to enjoy my childhood, at least when I wasn't doing chores. When he was the same age as I was on that day, he was in the Philippine Islands in

WWII, serving as a Seabee. So long as my grades were good he seemed to let me get by with playing hooky once in a while to hunt.

It wasn't a year later I was in college. Dad made a lot of changes. He got a self-propelled lawn mower. He bought a snow blower for the sidewalks. He even took out the wood furnace and installed a high efficiency natural gas furnace. He said he had to get those things because his workhorse moved out to college. The truth is that he made me go to college. I had pretty decent grades and he insisted that I go, even though I had no idea what I wanted to study. I majored in History and Anthropology, not the most employable degrees in the world. Who in the world would be foolish and desperate enough to hire someone with those diplomas? The church, that's who. Of course I needed a call and a couple more diplomas first.

I wasn't even a sophomore at Penn State yet when dad died. He had been battling cancer for over a dozen years. He had worked his whole life and used his vacations to work even more. I thank him for turning me loose in the woods so much and for teaching me about hounds and the wild things. I am also grateful that he was so insistent that I went to college, even though I didn't want to go. He firmly believed that boys needed all the responsibility that they could take and all the fun they could handle. Keep the cordwood stacked and dry, and keep the hounds running.

THE FOOD DRIVEN BEAGLE

Well, it had to happen. I was approached by someone who wants me to write a book. This is a person who watches too much cable news. Let me explain, this friend has made a full-time job of watching the news. Now don't get me wrong, I watch the news—I tend to read more newspapers than watch TV News—but I do watch the news. However, I do not plop in front of the cable news channels as if I were at some sort of buffet. I know lots of people who do this already and they keep me informed of the news propaganda that comes off the tube. I have friends who are wholly devoted to all of the major cable news channels. Some like CNN, others MSNBC, while others like FOX NEWS. Each picks his channel of choice based on political leanings. I don't watch any of these channels too much. I read several newspapers instead.

That being said, a while back there was a good bit of coverage devoted to the case where a fellow shot his way out of a courthouse, escaped the authorities for a bit, talked to a young woman he was holding hostage, and then surrendered. At the crux of the whole thing was the fact that this escaped defendant was convinced to surrender after his hostage read to him from a book called *The Purpose Driven Life*. When this all came to fruition, a person from church approached me and said, "Why don't you write a book that changes peoples' lives? Pastors are always writing books."

Why not? Hmm. I could write a book called *The Food Driven Beagle*. Much of my life revolves around the very real complications of owning dogs (i.e. beagles) that spend all of their time thinking about ways to get food. As I type this missive I am well aware that there are three beagles leaping and jumping in my kitchen trying to reach the food that has been placed above their reach. I am not kidding. I am six feet tall. I have fairly long arms. I have trouble reaching my food, that is the lengths, or should I say heights, to which I have gone to keep my beagles from overeating. Short people come to my house and cannot eat —they can't reach anything. All bread products are on top of my refrigerator. I have a hanging chain/mesh/metal basket that is suspended from my ceiling to hold my fruit. My house looks like a hunting camp in grizzly country—all food is secured.

I can't even store food on my counters. I have a Branko packed beagle named Shadow that is the smartest dog I have ever owned. He can easily clean the countertops of all the food stored there. That is why my fruit hangs from the ceiling, because Shadow loves grapes. He will eat grapes by the bunches. He also likes tomatoes. Shadow once pushed a chair across the kitchen in order to use it as a step to reach pasta sauce sitting in a pan on the stovetop. I have a picture to prove it. I kept hearing this noise—like a something solid was being dragged. I went to the kitchen to see Shadow on his hind legs pushing the chair with his fore legs towards the stove. I have friends who aren't that smart—they are my friends who jump around my kitchen trying to reach the fruit, they never think to get a footstool like shadow did for the tomato sauce.

I also store food in my oven and in the microwave. Left over pizza automatically goes in the oven (which is turned off, of course), and things like chips, potatoes, dry pasta, oatmeal and boxed rice all go in the microwave. This means that I have to unload the microwave to use it. Ditto for the oven. It can be a hassle. Where do I not store food you might ask? Well, let me tell you—*in* the refrigerator. This is because my hound dog Lady has learned how to get into that cache of food. She paws fiercely at the door of the appliance until it pops open. This has led to several terrible mishaps. She once ate 4 pounds of lunchmeat, cheese and hot dogs. On another occasion she ate a whole tub of butter.

Lady has also caused me great anxiety as I worry about potential canine poisoning. For instance, she once ate most of a box of chocolates, as well as the box. The vet said, "Let her pass gas and rest." She was fine, even though chocolate is poisonous to dogs. She also ate a whole onion. Onions are on the "do not feed" list for canines too. After a fitful vigil she had several bowel movements and was fine. The worst was when she broke into the refrigerator and ate 5 leftover chicken wings. I had nightmares of a perforated gastrointestinal tract killing my rabbit dog. When she became ill, a trip to the vet was required. $300.00 later (of course she ate the wings on a holiday weekend when the veterinarian rates are subject to exponential increases) the animal Doc confirmed, via very expensive x-rays, that Lady's stomach contained 5 very large turds, all lined up single file waiting to emerge into the world. She passed those fiery hot wings hunched over in pain as she sniffed the apples on the tree above her head, trying to figure out how to reach one. Even in pain her gluttony continued.

One thing my hounds do not touch is coffee. This has me worried. Because when I cook food these beasts lay on the kitchen floor waiting for any crumb that might fall. They are so ravenous that they eat before they identify. They will inhale the hottest of peppers, the most pungent of horseradish, and the strongest garlic, but they will not so much as place a tongue on coffee. This leads me to believe that coffee must not be any good for me, because my hounds will not only eat any and all food that falls to the kitchen floor, but they will also eat decomposed and decomposing flesh of any carcass found in the woods, various and assorted forms of fecal matter, and drink from mud holes that stink of agricultural runoff. How bad must coffee be for us if these same beagles won't hardly even smell a coffee bean that escapes to the floor?

Dog food is another matter entirely. It is kept under screw top lids in large heavy-duty storage bins. I have these storage bin lids tightened to the limit of my strength. Some folks who enter my house can't even open them. I once had somebody tend the hounds while I was away on vacation. It was an elderly lady from church. She couldn't open the dog food containers because they were too tight. She had to go buy more dog food. The containers were so tight because the same hound who opens the refrigerator also savagely attacks the containers of Purina until the lid rotates off the threads and onto the floor. Of course the well-intentioned church member left the 5-pound bag of dog food on the kitchen counter. Shadow knocked it down and the whole pack made quick work of the kibbles as they were strewn across the hardwood floor of the kitchen.

So, my book would have to be called *The Food Driven Beagle*. I doubt that it would save a life or end a hostage situation. I can see no real benefit that this book would provide to society. Well, the book might help people save themselves from paying a $300 x-ray bill.

MEATATARIANISM, LEFTY, AND PHIL

February is something of a special month in Pennsylvania. Groundhog Day is widely recognized as a day to celebrate the decision to allow a rodent—a hibernating rodent at that—to predict the weather. Punxsutawney Phil, meteorologist extraordinaire, is the star of the show. Doppler radar move aside, "We got us a woodchuck!" It makes you wonder what could have possessed people to seek meteorological forecasting from a sleeping whistle pig. Go to Punxsy once and see the size of the party. A party that big could convince people to ask investment advice from a lemming. Punxsy is a neat town and Feb. 2 is a good time to visit.

When I was a seminary student in Ohio, I remember that there was a spin off out there called Buckeye Chuck, who was based out of Marion, Ohio. I would think that a Cincinnati Sam, or a Mansfield Mike, or a Toledo Tommy, or a Cleveland Cliff would be a cool name for an Ohioan woodchuck, but Buckeye Chuck works. After all, if you are consulting a sleeping rodent, what does it matter what the name is? I am not sure if Buckeye Chuck has a large party crowd in attendance or not. I also am not sure if a movie has been made about Chuck, like the *Groundhog Day* movie. I do know that the critter exists, although it seems, to my memory, that Marion's popcorn festival, held in the summer, is the more important event. Punxsutawney does not have a popcorn festival. All of their eggs are in the February 2nd basket. They have not diversified into popcorn.

Anyway, it is something to do in the middle of the winter. It's a better option than succumbing to SAD (Seasonal Affective Disorder), the winter malady caused by shorter days that mental health experts tell us may be

responsible for the winter blues. Of course, extreme heat
and humidity cause tension and violence in the summer,
they say. If you work hard enough you can blame
everything on the weather. If you suffer from SAD, then I
recommend you go to Gobbler's Knob, in Punxsy for
Groundhog Day.

Why do I mention all of this stuff about woodchucks
and weather? Well, it is because my mind makes strange
jumps. Thinking of Groundhog's Day reminds me, quite
naturally, of groundhogs. Groundhogs remind me of my
first, and only, adolescent "fun job". I was sixteen-years-
old. A farmer was paying me three dollars for every
groundhog or woodchuck that I killed in his fields. A fly
fisherman was paying me two dollars for every groundhog
tail that I sold him. He made some kind of fly out of some
of the hairs on that tail. It was at that time that I thought
work must be the greatest thing ever. I was making five
dollars per woodchuck! Most of my friends were making
$3.35/ hour bagging groceries or even less for cutting
lawns for the summer. Work was fun! That exclamation,
quite logically, proved to be untrue for most jobs that I had
thereafter.

Being wrong made me think of being right. Right made
me think of left. Left made me think of my friend Lefty.
Lefty is one of those guys who is always on a diet. He
recently asked me about eating woodchucks, which brings
us full circle. Now, if I confused you, well just imagine the
misery that the flock I serve has to experience every
Sunday when I preach.

Anyway, back to Lefty. Lefty was always chubby. Some
might even say fat. That is a mean word, so I opt for the
term heavyset or sturdy. Who am I to talk? I ought to lose
about ten pounds myself. Or at least move it back to my
arms and chest where it used to sit. My biceps, triceps,
and chest muscles went south with the geese one winter
and just never came back. They actually seem to have
migrated to the Mid-Atlantic states, taking up residence at
my midsection. At any rate, those ten pounds of migratory
game muscle need to return North or be harvested in the
Mid-Atlantic. Lefty and I are friends and so I try to be
sensitive to his feelings.

I remember Lefty and I sometimes used to walk to school together. I tried to avoid walking with Lefty, which is just as mean as using the word fat, but sometimes it happened that we met and walked together. Lefty would stop on all the hills to catch his air. He had to pause going downhill too, it took some effort and Jake braking to keep Lefty from rolling free and wiping out a community of seventh graders on their educational commute. He was always late, and made others late too, which is why I tried not to walk with him. He was that far out of shape as a kid. He is still the only person I ever saw eat ten grilled cheese sandwiches and ten bowls of tomato soup and complain about every one of them. He grew more after graduation. But Lefty recently lost 200 pounds and he wants to lose fifty more.

Lefty accomplished this by becoming what I call a meatatarian. A meatatarian is the exact opposite of a vegetarian. Lefty lives on some diet that is basically meat. He buys special cookbooks on meatatarianism and he goes to meatatarian support groups. He is scared to see what his cholesterol is but he has lost weight. Once, he quit the meatatarian diet and gained 2 pounds per day. He says he is on it forever now. A sort of religion, I suppose.

Lefty was always a casual anti-hunter. What I mean by that is that he would wolf down three buckets of the Colonel's chicken and then bad mouth me for shooting a rabbit, squirrel or deer. He once had the audacity, while at a restaurant, to choose a swimming lobster, from a group of twelve or so in a tank, have it boiled and served to him and then tell me that passing up a small buck for a big one was malicious and cruel.

"Do you suppose that hamburgers are naturally boneless and wrapped in cellophane?" I asked at that lobster dinner.

"At least it wasn't murdered!" Lefty then scoffed that taxidermist mounts were a "Tacky display of sacred wild animals." And then he plowed into a pork dessert.

"Of course it wasn't murdered. It's a darn animal. Animals can't be murdered." I answered. "What is the difference between killing an animal on a farm and killing it in the woods? Do you think that all of those chicken wings you had as an appetizer came from young chickens that all died prematurely of natural causes?"

Lefty took off his leather jacket and stretched out his feet, tapping his leather shoes off the floor and thought about this statement. I was a little worked up at this point. Too many people cry over a road kill and are callous to human suffering. We agreed to disagree.

At any rate, that was the old Lefty. Now that Lefty is a meatatarian, he sings a new tune. He stops by my house all the time looking for new meat to add to his diet. It is as if the second I shoot a grouse, pheasant, rabbit, or deer, Lefty knows. It got a little ridiculous when I came home from a rabbit hunt with four rabbits and a grouse and Lefty was on my porch waiting for me, eating a bag full of beef jerky.

"Lefty, I liked you better as a fat man." I said, using the "F" word that I try to avoid around heavyset, sturdy people.

"But Ford, I can walk again. And I feel better, why would you say that?"

"Because you eat three-fourths of my game!" I growled, "Get your own hunting license! You run from corn like it was a hand grenade, potatoes like they were poison, and bread like it was the plague!"

"How else am I going to lose weight?!" Lefty sobbed.

"How about if you do some walking while hunting your own game!" I took the fresh food into my house and put it in my freezer. It was selfish, but I did it. It was a moment of tough love. Tough because I was afraid the guy might knock me senseless. Loving, because giving advice to hunt can hardly be viewed as hateful.

And Lefty did take up hunting. He took his safety course. He bragged about how well he did in the class. "I was the smartest one there. I know I have the best job of anyone there!" Lefty makes good money as a foreman of some kind.

"Lefty, the rest of the class was full of twelve year olds. What kind of job did you expect them to have?" I asked.

He kept losing weight, and he kept hunting. He missed more than he hit but he improved. He is so damn meat crazed that I never let him hunt with my dogs. I thought he might shoot one. Or get jealous when I feed the hearts to them. But he did shoot a few rabbits on his own by Elmer Fudding. Elmer Fudding is what I call the practice of stepping on brush piles and shooting rabbits in the hindquarters as they flee. Sure, you could do it that way, but it is kind of like putting a super strong engine under the hood of a hatchback or station wagon, or a minivan, what's the point?

Not long after Lefty started hunting, he stopped by my house to show me his license and his guns that he bought. He had completely read the game commission book from cover to cover. He read parts that I never read—like the season for woodchucks. I haven't hunted them in years.

"You ever eat woodchuck?" Lefty asked.

"I guess I have," I confessed. "A long time ago. Small ones aren't bad."

"You sure can hunt them a lot! It is a long season!" Lefty chimed.

"Say Lefty, why don't you go on a trip and do one of those moose hunts or something? That ought a tide you over if meat is all you want. There is a lot more to hunting than meat. Are all of you meatatarians this nuts—I mean, devoted?"

"I think I am more fanatical than some." Lefty answered, gnawing on a greasy, processed meat snack.

"Man cannot live on meat alone, Lefty" I said, hoping to persuade him to move down a notch on the food chain.

"That in the Bible, is it?" Lefty asked.

"Not exactly." I said I tried.

"I didn't think so. I am doing great on this diet."

Lefty was still eating mostly store bought meat but he was adding variety with the addition of what game he was able to shoot. Woodchucks became a favorite for Lefty. He found some young kid who liked to hunt them as I did those many years ago. That was last summer. Here we are in February. I can just imagine if Lefty went to Punxsutawney. They have Phil living in an enclosure of thick glass, stuck on the end of the library. As I recall, he is shacked up with some female groundhogs. I can see Lefty the meatatarian now, looking in at those woodchucks the way he drools over lobsters in a tank.

There is a sign in Punxsy that tells you that Phil is immortal. They claim to have been using the same woodchuck all this time. Like I said, it is a big party. Everyone ought to go once, just to see. I worry for Phil's immortality if Lefty is still a meatatarian. I am sure that any immortality status would have a clause in the insurance policy with a disclaimer that holds the right to revoke immortality privileges in the event of falling prey to a carnivore.

Maybe Lefty has forgotten about woodchucks, what with their winter hibernation and all. Recently he was by my house with the game commission book again.

"I see that there is a long season here for crows too."

"Yeah. Smart critters," I answered. "Hard to shoot."

"I think I might try to get a few." Lefty said. He was eating a BLT—minus the lettuce, tomato, bread, and mayo.

"I don't think anyone is going to recommend that you eat those things, Lefty," I cautioned.

"You are wrong. Haven't you ever heard the expression 'Eating Crow'?" Lefty reasoned.

"I guess I have heard that." I wasn't going to argue with him. Hey, he says he was the smartest one in his hunter's safety course. At least Phil is safe. Oh, and Buckeye Chuck.

"WHO WANTS TO BE A GUIDE?"

If you are anything like me, then you are perpetually inundated with mail order catalogues selling you outdoor gear. I get catalogues from the big stores as well as the little ones. I get a few that specialize in goods specific to outdoorsmen who own hunting dogs and I am always disappointed to see how little regard the upland hunters hold for our little beagle, as indicated by the sparse number of items for sale in their advertising specific to beagles or beaglers. I get catalogues for things I have no intention of buying—like bass boats. Daily I receive some advertising from some business.

Daily, is also the frequency with which I seem to curse at how dense some of those inch thick volumes of commercials can be, and therefore how difficult to burn. Page by page they must go into the burn barrel or else they will just smolder and smoke and leave glossy globs behind. Oh, but even if I have no interest in buying a thing that they sell, I can't burn a catalogue until the new one arrives. I could make a reasonable facsimile of a magazine rack with the catalogues I get. And it always makes for such a disaster at the post office.

You see I live in a small town, one that is so small that nobody with my zip code gets their mail delivered. Add to this the problem that the post office is not open yet when I start the workday and they are long since closed when I return. So...I try to get my mail once or maybe twice each week at lunch hour, presuming that I am in the area. And very often I have a yellow card from the post office indicating that I have a package. What could it be? A gift? Alas, I have to come back later, as no one is working behind the counter during the lunch hour in our little post office.

Coming back at another time presents its own obstacles. And heaven forbid that I have to return on Saturday. Saturday is the big day for all of us who work to come get our mail. There is a large population of retired people in our town and they can get their mail whenever they want to get it—although they still all go at the same time, that time being whenever those of us still working go to get our mail. Saturdays though, the place is a madhouse as all of the town's employed people plop in to retrieve their mail. We converge on that building like ants at a picnic—except we don't cooperate as much as ants do, we tend to compete.

Even though Saturday is the worst day, the rest of the week is no picnic. This is because everybody sits in their car and reads their mail, leaving no parking for newcomers to park their cars. This then forces the patrons of the U.S. Postal Service into a holding pattern. At any given time in my town of Ramey, you can see a steady stream of traffic circling the block of the post office, just waiting for clearance to land. And when I say clearance, don't be misled. There are no controllers. "Clearance" means that a car is pulling out. At that point various and assorted vehicles of many shapes and sizes all converge on the opening. The problem is compounded by the fact that there is only parking on one side of the road and people dive into these coveted slots on approach shots from both directions.

After all of that effort, and avoiding any claims on my auto insurance policy, I discover that my "package" is merely a bunch of catalogues too thick to fit in the box. But all is not lost. I can still tuck these catalogues away into my vehicle and save them for browsing later. Ministry is a combination of hurried bursts of activity combined with stretches of waiting. I have many days where I wake at 4 a.m. to go meet a family at a hospital for surgery at 6 a.m. and then we have prayers and tears followed by a long wait. Sometimes it takes 3 or 4 hours before the medical team even begins the surgical procedure. This is followed by waiting for the surgery itself and then waiting for recovery. This is when I will sneak out for a few minutes to get my book bag and buy a coffee and return to the waiting room. Then the catalogues come out. And lest you think I am some kind of rude pastor for doing this, let me remind you of a few things.

First, the reading material that I bring is decades more recent than anything the hospital has in their waiting rooms. I was in a waiting room recently and read an article on the Carter-Reagan election. None of the periodicals I bring are any older than one year and the vast majority are only a month old. Secondly, very little of the reading material provided by waiting rooms is geared towards the sportsman and that bit is already being read by somebody.

Lastly, people that I am there to see like these catalogues. When we are sitting through a five-hour surgery, it helps to have a little reading material there. People like a brief break from worrying about the worst-case scenario as their loved one is under the knife. So, out come the reading materials. The family members and I sit and plan fictional fishing trips and hunting adventures, outfitting our never-to-be-had vacations with never-to-be-purchased items from these catalogues.

After years of paging through these publications, I have come to this conclusion—somebody, somewhere, has decided that we will buy anything with the words, "Guide" or "Alaskan" on it. These advertisements are full of that stuff. Shirts, vests and compasses for guides. Maybe it is just me, but I think a compass made for a guide should be made to look like *anything other than* a compass. No one wants to see their guide holding a map and a compass spinning in circles muttering distress calls such as "Humph, well I'll be, how 'bout that" coming out of his mouth while scratching his head. But no, the guide's compass does, in fact, look exactly like a compass. A large compass; a big honking thing. Reality, I am sure, has the guide holding a GPS unit and a backpack full of batteries and spare GPS units stored in waterproof bags. The days of the compass in the pack of a guide must be numbered in this era of techno-hunting.

That is just my guess; I have never been on a guided hunt. Oh there was the time I approached this North Country farmer for permission to hunt hare, and he said, "I got no problem with it. Just go back there in those cedars. Your dog'll find so many tracks he won't know which way ta go." That is as close to a guided hunt as I have experienced, unless you count my first deer hunt at 12-years-old with dad when he said, "Just sit here until you get cold, then walk over there a hundred yards to where I am standing."

Maybe it's the fact that so few of us have been on guided hunts that encourage the advertisers to believe that we will buy anything with the word "guide" in its name. Coats, backpacks, boots, gloves, binoculars, and all kinds of things for guides. Maybe people buy this stuff thinking that they will wear this clothing and go into the woods to find a distraught hunter approach them for advice.

"Excuse me, Sir," a desperate sport would say to a hunter decked out in guide-gear, "I parked on the old fire tower road, just where is that from here?" The fellow, dressed in new guide gear, could produce a suitcase-sized compass and start spinning....

I suppose that is precisely the reason that I would not want the stuff. The last thing I want is people approaching me with the presumption that I know things. "Hello Sir, where are all the big bucks?" a chap might ask me.

"How the hell should I know, I haven't seen a legal buck in three years!" I would have to respond. And that is not a very guide-like thing to say. This, of course, brings us to the topic of expectations while wearing the guide caliber gear that is advertised in these glossy pages. For instance, if you are going to walk around looking like a cross between Indiana Jones and G.I. Joe then you had better be successful. It seems, however, that the guys I see wearing scarves, safari hats, outback khaki shirts, and cattle drover jackets never have any game in their vest or a deer dragging the ground behind them. I was in a restaurant in deer season—eating supper before going home for the night and not wearing my hunting clothes—and in walked a visiting hunter to our community. Most folks call these fellows flatlanders because they hail from the more flat regions and come here to hunt deer. They travel here from the Harrisburg area, Philadelphia, Midwestern states like Ohio and Indiana, and so forth. I personally do not like calling these pleasant visitors "flatlanders." Not only is the term meant to be cruel, but it is also inaccurate. A lot of these unskilled, dangerous, incompetent hunters come from the Pittsburgh area too, and that land is not flat. There was a hunting party on the adjacent hill from my hunting group this year that fired at least 100 rounds on the first day. They were shooting at running deer across an open field at ranges of 400+ yards. Hopefully they missed and didn't wound any. They either had a guy reloading shells in their camper or some store made a pile of money that night in ammunition sales. They were from the Steel City. They gave a bad name to all the great guys who were also visiting from out of town for deer season

Anyway, I digress. So this visiting hunter strolls into the restaurant wearing a scarf, a large pair of binoculars, several deer calls draped around his neck, and a hunting knife strapped to his leg that was only slightly smaller than Excalibur. I could tell right away that he fancied himself as a guide-type person. He had all the gear—including a belt-mounted compass and a smaller lapel compass pinned to his collar. He hadn't seen a deer all week but he was living proof that manufacturers of outdoor equipment are convinced that we will buy anything that is supposed to be utilized by guides.

And apparently that same advertising technique applies to any item that uses the word "Alaska" or "Alaskan" in its title. There are Alaskan parkas, Alaskan hats, Alaskan under britches, Alaskan down filled vests, specialty blades saws and axes that are—you guessed it—Alaskan and every other item that you can imagine.

Really shrewd advertising will go the extra mile and tell us that items are used and approved by Alaskan guides. Wow. The double shot of ego booster both Alaskan and a guide. It must work, however, because people make purchases of these items. I would be a liar if I claimed not to have anything that was advertised for guides or Alaskans. It must be designed to appeal to the little child in all of us that just wants to disappear into the mountains like the adventurers of olden times and leave civilization behind. It calls us back to those days as kids when we felt we could all become men of the hills and trap and pan for gold and hunt and live off the land. Anything good enough for Alaska has to be tough enough for the little patches of

winter-sport we call home. I honestly read of a piece of
equipment for Alaskan Guides that served as a walking
stick, shooting sticks, and repository for matches and a
compass. That is over the top just a bit. Now, if you will
excuse me, I have a card that claims I have a package at
the post office and I need to get there before they close. It is
either a bunch of catalogs or an Alaskan Guide quality
coffee thermos that I ordered a while ago.

GUNDOG BRACE: TO GO, OR NOT TO GO

Gundog brace. For many, the term itself is a bit of an oxymoron, with the emphasis on "moron." This is because of the bad taste left from the traditional brace movement. Now, I realize that there are beaglers who are not pleased with the term "traditional brace." The displeasure stems from an assertion that a traditional brace hound really could run a rabbit like the brace hounds of the 1950's. I refuse to listen to anyone tell me about hounds in the 1950's unless he was old enough to run and judge hounds of that day. So, a 20-year-old judge in 1950 would be an octogenarian today. Unless you are that old, then please, do not tell me what a brace hound is or isn't, or what a brace hound was or wasn't.

That being said, the term brace is packed full of negative connotations. It is hard to respect a movement that has added rules to determine what order hounds ought to be "laid on the line" in order to prevent owners from arguing over the coveted rear position. Brace beagling has not improved the beagle for hunting in decades. If you listen to brace beaglers you will hear conversations that exhibit great anxiety over the failure of brace trials to grow.

All that being said, I like the gundog brace format. I like it even more now that there is the option of running second and subsequent series in small pack. I think the gundog brace format emphasizes check work and it is difficult to hide a real faulty dog in a brace. Don't get me wrong, there are drawbacks to the format too—the first series can take you past lunch and approaching supper. You are less likely to get a second rabbit in a gundog brace trial then you are in a pack trial. The key is to pick and choose your gundog brace trials based on the club and the judges. A good judge is a good judge. The fact remains that there are two roads that lead to gundog brace—one road comes from the gundog community and the other comes from the brace community.

I have been to gundog brace trials and heard the words, "This is just like brace trials, only one step faster." If you hear these words at a trial, then you have wasted your time and money. In order to help you choose your gundog brace trials, I have compiled a list of various evaluative techniques and diagnostic tests that you can run to see if the GUNDOG is emphasized:

LOOK AT THE JUDGES

Most people look at the judges names before they travel but it is especially needed in gundog brace. AKC has some wonderful functions on their website. You can look at the future assignments of any judge. If you see a judge slated to judge a bunch of traditional brace trials as well as the gundog brace trial you plan on attending, then you will know that gundog brace trial is coming from the brace end of things and not the gundog side. I am also nervous about any judge who owns traditional brace field champions. Granted, there are a few converts out there who have abandoned the sinking brace ship and plunged into gundogs, but there are others who have a leg in two boats —and that isn't the place to be.

LOOK AT THE CLUB

You can look at a club and see if the club has two licensed trials. Some clubs will hold both a gundog brace and a traditional brace trial. To me, this tells you something about the type of gundog trial to expect. There are some notable exceptions and some clubs will run a great gundog trial and also a brace trial. By and large, however, a club's choice of format for its second licensed trial will tell the tale.

ASK FOR YOUR HOUND'S NUMBER WHEN YOU SUBMIT YOUR ENTRANCE FORM.

If you ask the field trial secretary for your dog's number and they give you a blank look, as if you just asked him to explain chaos theory and nuclear physics, then you are in trouble. I asked a field trial secretary for my dog's number one time and the guy just blinked at me for a full minute. I asked him a second time and he still blinked. I was beginning to think that he might be hard of hearing but he did manage to carry on a perfectly functional conversation with his assistant about a baseball game. A similar indicator would be whether or not a club uses hound names or numbers when setting first series. If the club uses the names for roll call only, and then uses numbers for rolling out the braces, then I am pleased. Other clubs, more traditionally rooted in brace, will read off each dog's name as the balls are rolled out of the cage. This method is done primarily, as far as I can tell, to ensure that everyone has an extra hour to eat breakfast.

START TALKING ABOUT TRIOS

As you probably know, a gundog brace trial has the option of running trios if the class has 30 or more entries (It may be different now, it has been awhile since I saw a class that large). What I like to do is walk around during breakfast and clap my hands and rub them together and say things like, "Boy oh boy, I hope we run trios today!" or "Hot diggity, there are enough entries here today to run trios!" These kinds of statements can reveal a lot about the people at the trial. If your fellow beaglers look at you with the same look that they would give to a bloated, road-kill deer, then you might infer that your colleagues are not too enthusiastic about seeing dogs really run a rabbit with enthusiasm and drive.

ASK ABOUT COLLARS

I prefer gundog brace trials that utilize the same collar colors as SPO trials. Many clubs do not use collars for gundog brace. I once was at a club that did not use collars and got rolled out as the third dog in a trio. Just for entertainment value I asked the field marshal for a blue collar. He gave me the same blank look that the field trial secretary gave me earlier when I asked for my dog's number.

DISCUSS CHECKS

One of the things that I like to do is causally mention check work. For instance, I once had the following conversation while waiting for my dog to run at a gundog brace trial:

"My dog routinely runs over the end of the line by 10 feet." This statement caused some rather shocked facial expressions.

"That's reaching pretty far, ain't it?" One fellow replied.

"Maybe. But a scared rabbit will jump 10 feet."

"A rabbit can't jump ten feet!" another protested.

"A scared rabbit can. I've seen it." I quickly found myself all alone. My statement of having seen a rabbit jump 10 feet seemed as incredulous as a claim to have once seen Bigfoot riding on the back of the Lock Ness Monster at Sea World.

Another litmus test would be to talk about "slotting up" and "wheel-barrowing." A very conservative set of judges will not allow a dog to advance to the front from the rear by any other means than slotting up, or moving ahead of another dog when the lead dog overruns a check. Slotting is seen as favorable in these conservative clubs.

Wheel-barrowing is what some folks call the process of remaining on the scent line left by a rabbit but doing it in a way that involves going right under the slower dog in front of it and turning it over. The fact that I have even learned the term wheel-barrowing should tell you that I have made the mistake of going to the wrong trial. I once had a dog jump over his brace mate at a trial. It sent the other dog's owner into apoplexy.

BE CREATIVE IN DESCRIBING YOUR DOG'S PEDIGREE

If you land yourself in a land populated by overly conservative gundog brace trials, then you will no doubt find yourself amongst many who have very strong prejudices. By and large, these ultra-conservative clubs will not look with favor upon a hound that has placed in hare trials. I always find this interesting, considering the fact that many of the folks in these cliques have never seen a hare or a "hare hound." You can mention the name of many a field champion that ultraconservative clubs have never heard. Smokes Creek Syris McGee—a great hound that is not known to these folks. Ditto for Melanson's Ranger Dan. The same could be said for Round Pond, Greenbrier, Fisch Creek, Dingus Macrae, or any hound from Little Ireland descent or with the kennel name of Adirondack. These are all great hounds that are unknown in the clique of pottering gundogs.

But the one name that these guys have all heard is Branko. Most have never seen a hound from Branko's breeding. Moreover, these guys could not name a single hound with the kennel name Branko. There are many great Branko hounds out there and the conservative end of gundog brace could not name one. All they know is that in their minds Branko means hare hound. This scares these guys. I am not sure what they are scared of. It could be the fact that they have never seen a hare—a sort of a fear of the unknown.

I like to create pedigrees for my hounds that test my colleagues at a gundog brace trial. What I do is create names of fictitious hounds that do not exist. It goes like this:

"Am I running in the next brace with you?" I will ask a guy.

"Are you in the fifth brace?" he will reply.

"Yep," I answer back.

"What is your dog out of?" The fellow asks.

Here is where I create hounds, "Well," I start, "I can't remember for sure. I think the top is Branko's Sight Chasin' Rabbit Eater and the bottom is a bitch from Branko's Run The Hare Until It Dies Of A Coronary. I think the third generation has a hound by the name of Branko's No Gun Needed, which accounts for all of its game by consuming the rabbit in mid stride."

This kind of pedigree fabrication is unethical to be sure and has caused great anxiety in many a beagler. One thing is for sure; this type of discussion can let you know if you went to the wrong trial. You can tell by the stuttering and loss of bladder control exhibited by your brace mate's owner after you get to the fifth generation of your fictitious pedigree.

PAINT

Paint is wonderful. Nowadays SPO trials all use the colored collars to designate the hounds in a pack. For some real fun, just splatter some paint on the sides of your dog. You don't even have to put the whole number, just some hints of previous numbers. Show up at an ultraconservative gundog brace trial with a dog that has a number on it and you are sure to cause a scene. Try saying this when you take your hound for pre-measure:

"I just got this hound back. I can't get all the paint washed off of him. He was campaigning in Maine and Vermont." If you want to really work these guys over, just mention the Canadian Maritimes. It doesn't even matter that they don't know what you are talking about.

TALK ABOUT RABBIT HUNTING

I like to ask folks at trials about their hunting season. If I get a lot of answers like, "There was too much snow" or "I didn't get a chance" then I know that I went to the wrong trial. I am always comforted by hunting stories from beaglers at trials. This is true even if they are half B.S. Any trial that is judged by guys who hunt rabbits will be better than one judged by guys who do not. That is the bottom line for me. Does this trial promote a hunting hound?

I hope that this has been informative and educational. Field trials are a lot of fun and can be even more fun if you try to enjoy yourself. Now, you will have to excuse me, because I am about to take my fun to the next level. There is a brace club (traditional) down the road that refused membership to me because "They did not know me well enough." I suspect the real reason is that they knew too much about me, considering they asked me only two questions:

1. What kind of dogs do you own?
2. Are they hunting dogs?

My answers, of course, were "beagles" and "yes." Presently, I actually do have one hound with some honest to goodness Branko hounds in the pedigree. Some Adirondack Bobby and Dingus Macrae too. I am soloing him lately because I plan on entering him in the traditional brace trial down the road. I hope that I am drawn second in my brace. Those boys will see some wheel-barrowing....

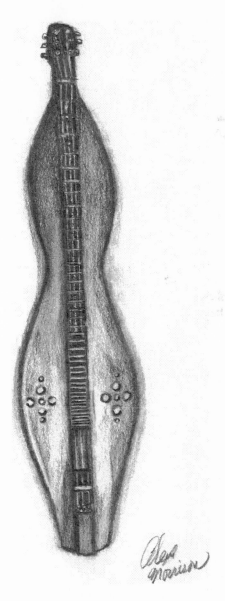

HI-TECH BEAGLING

Technology has made a great difference in the way that I hunt. Typically I am characteristically old-fashioned. My hobbies tend towards the low-tech end of the scale. I do not play video games, even though as a kid I belonged to the first generation of people to have game machines at home. My cell phone sits in the truck for emergencies, although usually the battery is drained. The computer is used for work and not very often for fun or entertainment. I still have not bothered with MP3 players or iPods. My favorite shotgun was made in 1929. I read books, paper books, and avoid computerized or digital books. I play the mountain dulcimer, an hourglass shaped musical instrument that has very old origins.

Recently, however, I have made a movement towards technology. All of it revolving around beagling. This all began when I was explaining to someone where I live. Ramey is not a large town—nobody gets their mail delivered. I try to walk to the post office, but that can be difficult; there aren't many sidewalks in Ramey. So, any walk in town is accompanied by coal trucks whooshing past as you walk along the narrow shoulder.

Inevitably, I will describe the location of Ramey in reference to State College or Altoona, neither of which is that close. On that particular day, I was talking to a friend in Pittsburgh and he began to use *Google Earth* to find the exact town of Ramey, and I dare say my house. This was fascinating to me. I went home and downloaded the same feature onto my computer—and started scanning the places where I rabbit hunt. I then started to look for similarities in the lands where I hunt. I was looking for the same sort of cover and color of vegetation and that sort of thing. Next, I started looking for comparable tracts of land in my area. I can't tell you that every spot that looked good on the computer was a rabbit paradise, but I must confess that more often than not the satellite photos proved very useful for finding great cover

Then I was hooked. I would hunt rabbit habitat on the computer at night and do a visual inspection the next morning. It was amazing. Do you realize how many roads have beautiful trees lining both sides for drivers to enjoy while the land a half-mile off the highway has been clear-cut and brushy cottontail cover has erupted everywhere? I was logging more computer time than I had in ages. My wife will often yell things like, "Get off the computer and come to dinner!" or "I told you to turn that computer off and go to bed!" These threats are commonplace, but they were never directed at me before—always at the kid! I am normally the person cussing at the computer because it is not performing in the way that I would prefer. Once, I even restrained the urge to throw a laptop through the window. But, there I was, being reprimanded for spending too much time online. It is a bit humiliating to have the teenager of the house wander past me and say things like, "Better not let mom catch you looking for rabbit cover."

Technology has also been added to my hounds. I saved up and bought one of the GPS collars to put on the dogs. That thing is amazing! It can tell you where the hound is and where it has been. It gives a bit of security when a beagle roars over the hill and into the next valley over. Naturally I have had shock collars for years and I have placed both collars on the same dog. It is an amazing thing to send a hound into the brush with all these electronic precautions. I can remember when the primary mode of retrieving a hound was leaving the hunting vest on the ground and returning after supper to find the wayward hound whimpering on top of the garment. It seems odd to walk into the brush, checking vest pockets for shells, patting the pants pocket to verify that a knife was brought, a quick tugging to confirm that the leashes are crossing the chest, and then reaching inside the vest to find all these hand held remotes dangling from the neck.

Another technological wonder comes to me by way of a gift. I received a pair of *Walker Game Ear* muffs for Christmas. They can provide sound amplification while simultaneously suppressing the loud crack of the muzzle blast. I already show signs of hearing problems. In church I have difficulty fielding prayer requests when I am at the pulpit. This is especially true for higher pitched voices. Sometimes my ears ring. The muffs work great. Although, I will warn you, those earmuffs can make a rabbit running through dry leaves sound like a herd of buffalo on a stampede! It takes a little while to adjust the volume so that you are hearing things at normal volume. I had to get accustomed to wearing the things but I am sure that I will be thankful later. We all know hunters who can barely hear. You walk into their houses and the high-pitched whistle of hearing-aides meets you at the door, the television is blaring and conversation is both heard and viewed as the old hunter watches your lips.

My hearing is not that affected. I can hear speech, but some words get missed. It isn't a perpetual problem yet and I can usually guess the word that I miss from the context. These muffs are doing wonders for protection. I was an old-fashioned nerd, the kind with books and mechanical pencils and things like that. I guess I am a Hi-tech nerd now. I can only imagine how I must look with all those hand held remotes around my neck and the big earmuffs on my head. If you think that is a nerd-fest, wait until you see the bicycle I am planning to build. I found a great place for rabbits on state game lands—located via *Google Earth*. The only problem is that the really good cover is five or so miles back into the game lands and the road is not for motorized vehicles. I plan to find a way to strap a dog carrier to a bicycle and ride in—I think it might look like the mean lady in *The Wizard of Oz* as she rides off with Dorothy's mutt in the basket—except even more bizarre due to the remotes and muffs. The problem is I can't get my dogs to ignore the first five miles of cover. They insist on beating the ground where there are no rabbits. Have you ever tried to move a dog five miles? It takes forever. A bicycle could take the dogs and me right into the prime cover. I'll have to let you know how the beagle-bike turns out. My other idea was to get a horse but I can only envision bad things happening there. I can hear the talk in the Ramey Post Office now, "That crazy preacher has a horse in that little yard. I saw him ridin' it with a dog in a saddlebag and all this stuff hangin' around his neck and a big set of earphones."

I got to go, my wife is yelling at me to turn off the computer.

HOME TURF

I brought home two rabbits one day from a quick hunt. I had been hunting an area that I know very well. I run dogs all year long and I value the rabbits that give my dogs hours of exercise, and provide hours of hound music for my ears. I have a couple of favorite places for these non-hunting jaunts afield. One of those places is literally less than half a mile from my house, as the crow flies. It isn't a large place and there are not "tons" of rabbit there, but throughout the spring and summer I develop a rather intimate understanding of these cottontails and their patch of real estate.

Rabbits might be born and die, and do everything in between, on just a few acres. And those rabbits *really* know their home turf. And they rarely leave it. The spot near my house is one in which I know the locations of all the groundhog holes that the cottontails will use for a getaway. I can almost always guess where the rabbits will circle and which way they will run. This familiarity is acquired by going there every morning for months at a time and observing hounds chase the local bunnies.

Within that little honey hole lies a boggy swamp that never dries—not even in the hottest part of summer, and it is in that bog and wet moss with all the tall weeds that my hounds and I will inevitably find a willing rabbit to chase in the months of July and August. There are a few clusters of apple trees that summon the rabbits in the late summer and early fall, and when the last of the goldenrod and tall grass are gone, there is a section of briars adjacent to a pile of tree tops mixed with the remnants of previous timber cuttings. This thick mixture of briars and tangled limbs hold the rabbits through the winter.

It would be safe to say that I visit that little tract of land 100 days each year, maybe more, and there are a few rabbits that I am sure I know personally. I know the way

they run and where they go and how to describe their
style. Yes, rabbits have style, at least some of them do.
Many beaglers tie their hounds in the back yard for 9
months out of the year and hunt them hard for 3. Others
run all year long. Those of us who pursue our sport both in
the gunning season and in the running season are drawn
to the chase and we can't help but take our beagles out
and see the excitement in their tails as they wag in feverish
fits of exhilaration and hear the overflow of that
exhilaration as they hark out and let their voices roll and
feel that desire as the hounds scurry in pursuit, moving
fast and with purpose.

And when you run rabbits everyday, you get to know
them in the same way that you know the route you take to
work. I started this piece by describing a day that I came
home from a short hunt with two rabbits. I knew those
rabbits as individuals. Taking one of those rabbits is
similar to butchering on a farm. It is the taking of an
animal that you have known. It is an intimate act, and
simultaneously one that firmly establishes a line of
demarcation between pets and food, livestock and animal
companions. A rabbit is designed to be eaten. Maybe by a
hunter, maybe by another predator, perhaps by a
scavenger, but a rabbit will be eaten.

Just as a rabbit will circle out of instinct, so too we
rabbit hunters return to the same hunting grounds year
after year, if not out of instinct then out of learned
expectation. I am no exception. I always hunt in places
where I have found rabbits in the past. And while I do not
know all of these grounds as well as my little spot next to
home, I do have a profound familiarity with each of them. I
know the vegetation and the topography and where the
woodchuck holes lie. I also know where to look for rabbits
in good weather and where to find them when it is
inclement.

Pursuing rabbits is different than hunting big game.
There is a successful bear camp close to my home. A group
of guys hunt there every year. They hunt with precision as
a team and they usually take at least one bear each
season, sometimes more. But it is done by pushing
through large expanses of land and not always the same

ground from year to year. It all depends on where bear have been seen.

I know hunters who go out west every year to hunt Elk. While they certainly go to the same general area, they may not step on the same trails as they did the previous year. Rabbit hunting, in contrast, is very much rooted to small pieces of earth. A beagler's roots stay in place. Our hounds are based out of a stationary kennel and our sorties afield are usually contained to day trips. Rarely does a rabbit hunter go off on a long trek to bag rabbits. Sure, some fanatics like me do, but by and large rabbits are a game species that is found pretty much everywhere—although not necessarily in equal numbers in all places.

Indeed, the very fact that rabbits are found everywhere is part of the magic. The pursuit of this game species is specific to place. And the hounds that are raised in those places are adapted to their geography. I own one hound from predominantly northern bloodlines. His hair is thicker, coarser, and just a bit longer. His drive is hard and fast. And while he may seem to have too much foot at times, he is right at home in 3 feet of snow. Likewise, if you want to run in the Deep South, you want a dog that will not overheat. There are many hounds that can run in all conditions and I do not want to give the impression that every region of the country raises different beagles, but it is worth noting that location shapes the hunt, and location shapes what we view as desirable in a beagle. Beagling is about running *your* dogs whenever *you* can and doing it on *your* home turf.

Rabbit hunting is very much about rushing home from work and getting the dogs afield for those last couple hours of daylight. Or beginning the morning with a quick hunt before going to work for the day (if you work second shift.) Rabbit hunting is something that is woven into life. It can be done with little or no preparation, it is a sport enjoyed in a very organic way.

Do you want proof of how connected beaglers are to their place? Ask one about what has to be done to go on vacation. Arrangements have to be made to get someone to clean the kennels and tend to the needs of the hounds. Vacations provide a time away, but beaglers who are truly connected to the chase will inevitably spend the hours of a return drive home thinking about taking rover out and running a rabbit.

So where am I going with all of this? I am looking at the reality of the chase. Old running and gunning grounds go away. They are consumed by stores and parking lots and houses. New places arise, sometimes in the midst of consumption. A strip mine is one of the ugliest things you can see. But give it some years and it produces rabbit habitat that is ideal. Ditto for forest fires. Clear cuts foster the growth of underbrush and provide another source of cover.

The rabbit is an amazing rodent. It knows its home and knows every corner of it. The same is true for the hunters that chase them. We too know their home. It is also our home. It is a sport of locale, place, and spot. Our eyes look for the particular and the specific. We hunt small game. Most of the major outdoor magazines talk about hunts for antlers that take place hundreds or thousands of miles from home. And that is good. Those hunts are O.K. by me. I wish I could go on one. Bunny hunting is less about distance and more about home. Not so much about there, everything about here. It takes a local piece of ground and elevates it to the status of special. In a world where overpopulation, overgrazing, overproduction, and other land uses prefixed by the word "over" is rampant, there is nothing more needed than elevating land to a status of being special.

I cleaned those two rabbits from my local spot and have on many occasions returned to run others that I am sure were descendants. I can still see the places in my mind's eye where the shots rang out that brought home the game. I can see those places in such detail because I am there so very often. I respect the little rabbit and his home. I am grateful for being allowed to share space with him. He has taught me that land is special; even the land that I see every day, or should I say, *especially* the land that I see every day. I am no scientist and not a philosopher either, but I do believe that we can learn something about how to manage the land. Maybe if we worry about the rabbit and the other game that lives where he does, the land that is near and commonplace, we will have the beauty of the natural world for generations to come.

HONEY HOLES: THE ART OF HUNTING HALF OF A MORNING

I do a lot of traveling. It goes with the territory of being a pastor. I frequent many hospitals and nursing homes. This mobility allows me to find a lot of honey holes to hunt. Without a doubt, hunting holes comprise the vast majority of my outings in pursuit of Peter Cottontail. Perhaps I should define what I mean by the term honey hole....

There is a common perception that goes something like this: preachers only work one hour each week. It is a misunderstanding, to be sure. But, the truth of the matter is that a pastor can adjust his or her hours in a way that allows for more work to be done in the morning or more in the evening. During rabbit season it is not uncommon for me to hunt for a couple hours every morning and make it to work a little late; somewhere between 9am and 10am. If I decide to do these half-morning hunts, it requires that I go to a honey hole, a few acres of land that is located pretty close to home, which provides a home for a few rabbits. In a quick couple of hours I have time to get a few rabbits up and running. Sometimes I come home with an empty game bag, once in a while I get the limit, usually it is somewhere in the middle.

And I will pass on this one little hint to anyone who hasn't already figured it out: cemeteries. I spend a lot of time at cemeteries—for work and for rabbits. If you talk to any pastor, you will be able to find a story about a funeral procession that left the hardtop and ventured into some ancestral cemetery which measures just a little over a couple acres and contains just a handful of grave markers. It is on these ventures when a pastor can be riding in the lap of luxury in the Cadillac when the funeral director (or the associate) will grip the steering wheel and say, "Hold-on" as the luxury car fishtails up a skid road to the place of the committal service. If you have never had the experience of hearing a dignified, professional funeral director wearing a designer suit caution you to "hold on" then you have missed out on something. And few moments are as hair raising as when you are snaking up a ridge on a narrow precipice and the driver of the Lincoln Town Car looks at you wide-eyed, sweat running down his face and asks you, "How much room is on your side?" It is moments like this when hearses get muddy.

It is rare to see a filthy, mud-splattered hearse. They do not usually come in off-road packages. Most hearses are shiny and spotless. But if you see a muddy hearse you can rest assured that it is on its way to a car wash, having just crawled off a road used only by the bravest log-truck operators. I once got to drive a Cadillac after a funeral on a nasty winter day. Few people can claim to have "rocked" a hearse out of a ditch by shifting between forward and reverse in rapid succession and then navigated it back to the paved road.

And many of these remote burial grounds are maintained as well as any golf course in the world. It is rather amazing really. Funeral associations spend gobs of money to ensure that their sanctuaries of rest are groomed and respectable. Scattered around the periphery of any rural cemetery, you will find thistles and brush piles which have been hacked and trimmed and timbered into the background in order to allow for a clean cemetery. It is a band of scrub and thistles that separates the groomed cemetery from the wild woods, a swath of semi-maintained real estate that forms prime rabbit cover. And there are rabbits there! Often there are not many, but always a few. Cemeteries are among my favorite honey holes. Not that I want to give the impression that I walk amongst the tombstones with a semi-automatic shotgun blasting away at rabbits as they slalom through the tombstones in an irreverent disregard for the dead. Quite the contrary, the hunting takes place in the brush and briars which are on the outskirts.

There are other honey holes as well. Small strips of land that the owner decided to have timbered for money, in extreme cases hacking the land down to where every tree capable of yielding a toothpick was harvested. Or those areas where a brushfire broke out and claimed a corner of the woods for small game and songbirds. And in my vehicle, I always carry a pair of coveralls and boots. Winter provides great opportunities for locating new honey holes. I have been known to pull off the road on the way home from a meeting and throw some Carharts over my dress clothes and wade into the briars looking for fresh rabbit tracks in the snow,

All of these little honey holes provide for great hunting. A short drive into the woods, a hurried chase, a fleeing rabbit, and a hound or two in pursuit provides the ideal way to start a morning. The early morning is then capped off with a quick change of clothes and a dash back to work.

Honey holes are where I always take first time rabbit hunters. I took Norm rabbit hunting to a honey hole one day this year. Norm is a fanatic about hunting. He is forever telling stories about exotic hunting trips to Canada (note to Canadian readers; Canada really is exotic when you hail from Pennsylvania), or to the Rockies, or even overseas. He talks about big game and bigger game. Once in a while he will commit himself to turkey, but Norm could never find any appreciation for hunting small critters.

I took Norm out one day to a favorite honey hole. We took just one dog. When I go rabbit hunting with first time hound hunters I always use one hound and about 9 bells. I want that dog to sound like a whole bell choir as it walks through the woods to ensure that it isn't shot.

"Where are you taking me?" Norm asked as I fishtailed up a rutted road off of the blacktop.

"To my favorite hunting spot," I answered, "How much room you got over there?"

"Go your way! Go your way!"

"Relax Norm, I had a Cadillac up here once, this will be easy."

The road widened and I parked. "What kind of sicko are you, Ford? This is a cemetery," Norm gasped.

"I know," I said, "And it is a really good one too. Be careful getting out on your side. It is a long way to the bottom."

We went about hunting and soon Norm forgot all about the fact that we were in a cemetery. "Seems like a lot of work for such small amounts of meat." Norm grumped as he loaded his gun."

And all at once the woods erupted as one lone beagle began to chase. Up and down the hills and around the brush and across the creek and back again he raced. Over and over again the dog came by and we never seemed to be in a position to see the rabbit. Norm began to brim with excitement. Big game hunting fueled his hunting dreams but here he was less than 10 miles from home and he was thrilled. No doubt about it, a 13-inch beagle can make it sound as if he is involved in a hunt of tantamount proportions. That little dog can lead you to believe that his quarry is the king of the forest.

And I suppose in many ways the rabbit is the king. If an animal eats meat, then it eats rabbit. Ground predators, air predators, and scavengers eat them. Red squirrels, I am told, will even eat the young bunnies in the nest. In the world of carnivorous Mother Nature, the rabbit is the foundation of the food pyramid and so I guess hunting rabbits could be viewed as an epic struggle.

BOOMBOOMBOOM! Norm's gun erupted. "Coming your way!" he yelled.

I never saw the rabbit as it squirted through the brush. The dog came through, though, and he jingled and jangled like a tambourine in the process. *BAM BAM BAM*! "I missed again!" Norm yelled, "There's another one! Hey, there is more than one rabbit in here!" Norm continued in excitement, pointing out the obvious.

We jingled and jangled through the morning. Everything went well and we managed to get a few rabbits. We quit when Norm ran out of ammo. I, of course, did not run out of ammunition. I carry a spare box of shells in my vehicle with my lunch. Norm will learn that trick. We eased back down the road and into town, leaving the cemetery behind. Cemeteries are wonderful markers of time. Generations of a community find their resting spot there.

And in the thickets off to the side, the generational struggle of Mother Nature takes place as well. The wily rabbit shakes and grooves and twists and turns, just as its ancestors have for generations. No antlers, no hides, no spurs or beards to parade as a trophy from the rabbit.

I left a cemetery this year and quit hunting because I saw people setting up for a service. I had a young fellow from church hunting with me - a high school senior who's name is Doug. He grew up in a home with beagles. His grandpa, who passed away a year or so ago, was a beagler.

"Maybe we should go," I said, "Looks like a service, I'm sure that they do not want to hear barking dogs during it."

"Probably not," Doug said, "But I bet that Gramp would have preferred his service be that way. He sure loved beagles"

"Yeah, I am sure he would have."

Another generation finds its rest and the rabbit and the hound still continue their struggle. It is good to be a part of that. And no one ever seems to notice that I sometimes go to work wearing boots with my slacks.

JUNKYARD DOGS

I was nervous as I listened to the rings in the phone, waiting for an answer. Finally, after seven agonizing rings, a "Hello?" came back through to my ear.

"How is she, Doc?" I asked.

"Not good. Bleeding real bad, and lost pressure almost entirely."

"What do you recommend?" I asked.

"Better come in quick. We'll talk when you get here."

Up the long, twisted township road I crawled. Past thickets of briars and brambles—familiar ground that I have hunted in the past. I crept cautiously, not wanting to damage the undercarriage of my sedan. I nosed up the driveway and eased to a stop. I walked in the door.

"Hey, Ford. Doesn't look good here," Doc whispered.

"Can I see her?"

"Yeah, come on in." He led the way through a doorway and into a large room with all the equipment his profession required.

"What's the verdict?" I asked through teary eyes.

"The verdict is you drive like a damn madman!" Doc shouted, "You have no one to blame but yourself."

"But...but...b-b-b...I didn't hit anything. I was careful...."

"But without a transplant, this girl has had it. She has low compression. Her valves are leaking bad."

"And so..."

"You need a new engine in this thing!" Doc said, wiping down his *Snap-on* tools with a clean rag and dropping my 1978 Toyota's hood shut with a thud.

"She's been the best hunting rig I ever had. I've had her for seven years now. And that Chevy small-block 400 has been the greatest."

"Too great for you, lead foot. You have worn that girl out running over all the hills and dirt roads and snow covered lanes you can find in pursuit of rabbits!" Doc tells it like it is. He holds nothing back. He is the best mechanic you could hope for. He has repaired almost everything on my vehicle - even fabricated cross-members from tubular steel and floor panels from 14-gauge steel. Doc is my age. He's been working on cars since before he can remember. His dad owns the business—a body shop/mechanical repair/salvage yard. Doc was in the garage since he was a toddler.

I needed to think about my poor Toyota. I walked out of the garage bay and into the field of cars that lay before me. I startled two pups in the salvage yard. There are rabbits everywhere. They live in the goldenrod, briars, and tall grass that grow in patches between and amongst the cars. I remember Shadow and Rebel both had their first rabbit taken here. I was always allowed to hunt there but only with a .22 caliber rifle. The owners of the salvage yard did not want me shooting any car parts. Their theory was that a wide spreading pattern would hit cars. A little .22, properly aimed, would not. They were expert shots themselves and competed in marksmanship contests. The presumption they made was that all of us shoot that well with a rifle. I always worried about a ricochet if the little rifle ever missed the mark, but it never occurred.

Shadow was a wicked fast pup, and I still remember the day that he bounced his first cottontail out and almost caught it. The rabbit bolted across a field and tried to run in a straight line to the timber on the other side of the pasture. Shadow locked on that rabbit in a sight chase and quickly showed that he could run faster than a cottontail. He caught up to his quarry just before reaching the edge of the field and rolled the rabbit; but the bunny made it, scared but uninjured, to the safety of the woods. When it came back to me, slinking through a mass of station wagons, it had come to a stop and was sitting by a pile of scrap tin when I shot it.

Rebel was another story. He flushed his first harvested cottontail out of goldenrod that grew between an old Ford and a pile of hubcaps. It ran past an informal gathering of rear axles and emerged in a clearing and paused. I put the .22 on the vitals of the rabbit and squeezed the trigger.

The rabbit took one last spring with his powerful hind legs and crawled under an antique Pontiac. I could see it lying there dead but could not reach the bunny. The old car was lying on the frame rails and was hard to reach under. You remember frame rails don't you? They date to the time before they invented unibodies, back when they made carburetors. You know, when the high/low beam switch was on the floor.

Anyway, five-month old Rebel came through and crawled under the car and proceeded to start eating *my* rabbit! He didn't come out until he had a belly full of the source of the scent that he loved so much. I was finally able to take a stick and sweep under the car and retrieve what was left of the rabbit. There wasn't much there. Rebel walked down a dirt road with a puppy belly packed full of meat.

I sure love that old junkyard. Doc was in the garage with my ailing hunting vehicle and I was still wandering the aisles of cars. I walked by an old FJ-40. It was sitting on its axles. The vehicle donated a lot of parts to my own FJ-40 over the years. Both door handles, a seat, a windshield wiper motor, a starter, transfer case, and universal joints. I liked to think the old wreck was happy to donate to a working vehicle. But that was looking like a thing of the past.

"Hey, Ford!" Doc's voice rang through the air. "Get in here!"

I slowly inched back to the garage, afraid to face the inevitable. I walked into the bay and looked at my mule. I call her mule because as the original Toyota parts break I replace them with GM. Just as a mule is part reliable donkey and part flashy horse, so too is my metallic mule part sturdy off-road Toyota and part raw, Chevy horsepower. There are lots of miles and lots of trails on that old gal.

"I hate to put her down," I said.

"Fine. I have an engine you can get cheap."

"I can't put it in. I am not that good with tools, you know?"

"Oh, I know," Doc said. "I remember the dog box you made." Doc fought to suppress laughter.

"I'll put it in for free. But don't tell no one. It ain't no new engine either. And it ain't gonna last you forever. So you better not hoss on it like you are prone to do..."

Doc would take out the 400 and replace it with a 350. The 350 would cost me a couple hundred, but the labor was going to be free. He said he would charge me to rebuild the 400, however, if he did it slow and when he was in a good mood, he would give me a discount on labor. It would be ready when the 350 gave up the ghost.

That was last year. Recently, on a cold January morning, Doc and I walked into the salvage yard with Rebel. We each carried one of the new .17 calibers in place of .22s. Nice guns. They have a tiny bullet that will group inside of a nickel at a hundred yards. Inside of a dime at 125 if you're Doc. It is the only place I use a rifle to hunt rabbits. We shot our limit in short order. All of them out on the paths that wind in and out of the cars. The rabbits tend to get out on the paths and wait for the dog to squeeze out through the vehicles. They sit statue still, often 75 yards away from the hunter, and even further from the hounds. The dogs would crawl and fight through the cars and briars and the rabbits might jump out well over a hundred yards in front of the dogs and pause.

It seems too easy. But Doc doesn't think so. He is a mechanic by trade but loves to garden. I sometimes have to hold back a laugh when he towers over me and in his gruff voice explains the beauty of certain flowers that he and his wife. They also plant a vegetable garden and the rabbits are public enemy number one. Luckily, I am invited to come back every year and help control the rabbit population that has ample cover from the predators.

Down to the garage we went to clean the rabbits. We placed the entrails in a garbage bag and the meat went into a huge bucket of salt water.

"Thanks for saving my mule," I said.

"Don't mention it." Doc plopped a neat rabbit into the bucket and paused to rub Rebel's belly. Doc had lots of little dogs running around the garage. They are dogs with longevity; most of his mutts live to be well into their teens. God knows how they avoid being hit with all the traffic up that remote driveway to the garage. But they seem to

manage. Doc finished rubbing Rebel's belly and went over
to the barrel stove that heated the garage. He cut two
bloodshot front legs from two rabbits, deboned them, and
threw them into a pot. He boiled the meat right there on
top the barrel stove while we sat and talked. When they
had cooked through he ran them under cold water to cool
them fast and fed them to Rebel. "He likes that," Doc said,
"Good thing you shoot bad so he can eat."

"Whaddya mean? I didn't miss any," I protested. Doc
laughed as he sipped steaming coffee. All of Doc's rabbits
were shot in the head.

"I know you didn't have to fix my vehicle," I changed the
topic, "I also know that I couldn't have afforded the labor to
pay you."

"Well," Doc said, "I kinda like the look of disgust those
soccer moms get when they hear you coming in that beast.
And I love telling them that you're a pastor who drives like
a dirt track hero."

That was a little friendly insult. Doc's the real dirt track
racer. He has trophies to show it from local race tracks. I'd
like to know about half of what Doc forgot that he knows.
But I am grateful that he is my friend. And he helps me
out. I said goodbye to Doc and Rebel and I walked toward
the Mule. Her used 350 was still motoring strong. I knew a
stronger 400 would be waiting when the time came. I
carried most of four rabbits in my hand—tucked into a
gallon Ziploc bag. Rebel carried the rest of the rabbit,
tucked securely in his belly. His stomach wasn't swelled up
with meat like it was that day when he was five months old
but he still had that happy puppy trot. I love this salvage
yard.

SPIRIT OF THE LAW

As a clergyman, I suppose I should be well versed in matters of law and grace. My own theological stance is one where grace ought to allow the spirit of the law to breathe life into ethics. This is not to say that the letter of the law is bad, but rather that I am not so inclined to be that picky about the question where intent is good and bad results are minimal. This mindset that I employ even applies to hounds and I tend to accept things that the practitioners of strict adherence to the letter would not tolerate.

For instance, a seasoned hound will become what we always called "rabbit-wise." A young hound may function on pure physical ability and raw muscle. An old dog might use wisdom to make life a little easier. It has always seemed to me that the freezer gets full faster when a hound has acquired rabbit-wisdom and still has a body young enough to hunt hard—this attainment of rabbit-wisdom can often happen even in a young hound, and I have always felt that a diet high in protein and even higher in rabbit tracks run solo can yield a rabbit-wise beagle at a young age. I run my hounds in a pack for my ear but solo for their improvement with the basic assumption that any hunting beagle that can't solo a rabbit has nothing to offer the pack. That being said, I have kept jump dog specialists who contribute little after the rabbit is up, and a few check-work wizards that have managed to run a line relentlessly on very poor scent but struggle to jump a rabbit on a dew-soaked morning.

At any rate, there are violations of the letter of the law that I tolerate in the name of grace. Skirting is one.

Skirting is a fault, and I am not talking about a real severe case, but I have found that it is very common for a rabbit-wise hound to chase up to a small brush pile and circle it quickly to ensure that the bunny hasn't already left the premises and finding no scent then dives into the pile.

Don't get me wrong, I am not talking about avoiding an acre sized clump of greenbrier but rather a pile of dense interlocked branches and potential cordwood heaped in a pile the size of a living room. I have had dogs picked up or suffer demerit heavily for this sort of skirting under certain judges. I feel grace should prevail for the rabbit-wise hound.

Swinging is another. I don't like to see a dog hook out 50 yards but a rabbit-wise beagle will learn to use his eyes. A beagle can get to a check and see a rabbit trail tunneling into the underbrush and then follow it. Such guessing can be very flawed, especially in beagle clubs and enclosures where there are rabbit trails everywhere but in the wild, where I usually run, the rabbit population has not created as many trails and an experienced hound can guess well. Sight chases are not limited to times when the beagle can see the rabbit! My best snow dogs have all been cheaters looking for tracks on the powder with their eyes. I let the spirit of the law prevail here.

Please understand that I am no opponent of the standard. I hate to see skirting and swinging, I am just saying that I appreciate the rabbit-wise hound that seldom looses a rabbit. Besides, the letter of the law is dangerous in its own right. I suspect that a misunderstanding of the letter of the law in regards to the desired quality of accuracy while trailing had some contribution to the creation of the traditional brace beagle. Likewise, an overzealous letter of the law reading on the demerit of pottering has led to a few instances where all the dogs solving checks were eliminated, leaving a winners pack unable to circle a rabbit—although what chasing does happen is very fast!

As I write this, it is New Year's Eve. I am on vacation with my family visiting seminary friends. We left for vacation a day late. You see, my wonderful wife was packing in the morning and we were supposed to leave after dinner (that's lunch for lots of people) on Wednesday (December 29th). She gave me permission to hunt and to skip dinner but she said, "Don't hunt till dark or anything." Well, I had a rabbit wise-dog on good snow and the chases and the bunnies just kept coming! I ended the hunt at 4:50 p.m. on a rabbit that had spent well over an hour running with more wisdom than I had, managing to always present itself at 50+ yards away. The cottontail was not more rabbit-wise than Rebel, who kept the line between his legs, guessing a few trails, looking for fresh footprints, and skirting a bit of logs at a spot that was once a lumber mill. The rabbit finally showed himself in range and the last bunny of the afternoon was put in the vest. I took the dog to the truck, got the cell phone out of the console, and called my wife.

"What?" she answered in a voice that clearly indicated she had read the caller I.D. and was not pleased.

"I'm done hunting," I replied in a voice that was intended to sound innocent and chipper. Silence was her response and then a sigh—the kind of sigh that conveys disappointment, displeasure, and disgust more clearly than any verbal communication. I debated what to say next and foolishly landed on the question, "What's wrong?"

My wife is an ordained clergywoman and you would not believe the bad words that she knows. I got an earful about how I was still an hour away, we were leaving late and having to drive in the dark, fear of hitting deer at night, and how I should not have even gone hunting on a day we were driving four hours. She ended her condemnation by saying "I told you not to hunt until dark!"

I turned to the west and saw a gorgeous sunset, the top of the sun still visible on the horizon as it cast a warm glow on white snow. I looked at the tired dog lapping water and calmly said in the phone, "It's still light out." She hung up. We left early the next morning to visit friends. Clearly the letter of the law got me in trouble. It was *not yet dark* when I quit hunting. I am hoping that grace returns and I get a kiss at midnight to ring in the New Year. She is shopping at the moment. I said she could shop until well after dark if she should so choose.

MARRIAGE: KNOW ONE
TOWEL FROM ANOTHER

Looking back over the Februarys of my life, I have come to a few conclusions. First, there is nothing romantic about this month. It is absolutely gray and cold, or perhaps wet and chilly with that ugly snow that is melted and mixed with mud and dirt and cinders. January is more romantic; it, at least, is cold beyond belief and encourages fireplace evenings. But February is neither winter delight nor spring renewal. It lacks winter zest and has no springtime frivolity, which makes February a great time to talk about marriage, rather than new love.

Secondly, even if February reeked of romance, it is still a month of hunting season and for that reason is disqualified from any romance that involves daylight planning or excursions. Again, February is a great time to talk about marriage. A number of years ago I proposed to a young lady and she foolishly decided to accept. Ah, and in September of that year we took the plunge. This month I thought that I would share some of the things of marriage that really matter when a sportsman ties the knot. After all, a sportsman or sportswoman is subject to all of the typical afflictions that plague any other person but our odd personality flaws have particular forms.

For instance, did you know that some towels are allowed to be used for drying one's hands and others are not? Honestly, that is true. If you are shocked, rest assured, I am too. I mean, granted, I have decorative things as well. For instance, my father's battered hunting coat. But it is in a box stored away—not hanging in a closet where it has the appearance of being available for use in the field for a hunt.

Here is the challenge for the married man—towels that are purely decorative are always found hanging next to towels that are for regular use. Furthermore, there is no label to help you decide which towel is for use and which is a museum piece. Oh, and these towels are everywhere—below the kitchen sink, in the bathrooms, on the kitchen oven handle, in the laundry room—there may be a few in the garage, I don't know.

Now, for those of you who have not learned this, let me share a warning that should be heeded by you men as keenly as any rodent hearkens the ear to the cry of a Blue Jay or the bark of a squirrel—wives periodically swoop through houses like hawks and feel the decorative towels for any hint of moisture or ruffled appearance. I have, in my opinion, learned the secret to a happy marriage—learn which towels are off limits and stay the hell away from them. In particular, never assume that any towel, no matter how small or threadbare, is allowed to leave the house to test the oil level in your car. If you do "steal" a towel for checking your oil, do not leave it anywhere where it can be found—for instance beside the garage door.

Now, I am sure that there are other things that have to be done for marital bliss. Marriage experts will go on and on about the need for *understanding* and *communication* and *openness* and the need for *sensitivity* within a relationship. Those experts are, in fact, somewhat accurate. You need to *understand* which towels are off limits, you need to clarify your suspicions of these towels by *communication,* be *open* to the very real possibility that some towels—without warning—will be moved from the category of utilitarian to the category of decoration, and be *sensitive* to the reality that you may need to just dry your hands on your pants when you are unsure.

"Did you use the towel on the right side of the sink?" my wife asks.

"Yes honey bunny, that was the side you told me to use."

"No, I told you to use the blue towel with the white inlay, not the white towel with the blue inlay."

"Right, the towel on the right."

"I switched them Saturday."

"Oh...sorry."

"Remember some towels are for show."

I would hate to leave you with the impression that I have no domestic faults. In fact, I have many. One of them is that I spend way too much time in bookstores. I quit going to libraries when bookstores started allowing me to drink coffee while reading books I have no intention of purchasing. I simply go into the store, drink a hot cup of Joe, and read a few chapters. I leave the book on a table and return to finish the text in a few days.

I used to think that I was a lucky customer at my local Barnes and Noble. You see, I always was able to go to the sporting section of the store and walk over to a soft, padded chair on the other end of the store. I could never figure out why the chair was always available. No one was ever in it. That is, until my adoring wife pointed out that the chair sat in a section of books devoted to self-help and sexuality. No one wanted to sit in that section and look like a loser with personal problems too deep to comprehend. I didn't care; it beat standing up with a book in one hand and a cup of coffee in the other.

But it isn't the reading of books that gets me in trouble. It is the purchasing. Granted, I read way more than I buy but sometimes I just can't resist. For instance, I just bought a copy of *On Killing: Meditations on the Chase*, edited by Robert F. Jones. It is a great collection of essays on hunting and what it means to kill our own food. The Barnes and Noble lady at the cashier's stand was nervous when she read the title of the book but I have come to expect this from many in the book-business. The troubles at home can be worse when I arrive home with yet another book. I try to explain that the book was a stray and followed me home, but it never seems to work.

My wife is a true outdoorswoman though. She loves to train hounds and loves to get outside and chase any game I might be after. A pretty fair cook of game too—she has many terrific recipes for game of all kinds. And I can't tell you how many places she has found to hunt by getting permission from the Lady of the house.

"You can ask Farmer Brown until you are blue in face," she once told me, "but it isn't really Farmer Brown who wants hunters off the land. It is Betty, and she is still mad about the boys from Philly who shot a deer in her barnyard last year. But she likes me and we can hunt rabbits on the back fence row anytime."

Yes, married life is treating me pretty well. Our worst arguments have always been over towels. Oh, there was one other heated discussion. It was shortly after matrimony and it involved the time that she saw my guns. Apparently she felt that all hunters had one shotgun and one rifle, just like she does.

"What do you do with all those guns?"

"I use them."

"No you don't."

"Yeah I do. I have that deer rifle there."

"Right, the only one you use."

"I use the other one with open sights when it is raining hard."

"You don't hunt when it rains hard."

"I have a couple shotguns for various occasions"

"You only use the one."

"The .17 is for squirrels."

"What about the .22?"

"I used to use that one for squirrels."

"How 'bout the muzzleloader? You don't even hunt muzzleloader because it conflicts with second season small game?"

I was starting to struggle a bit—and then it came to me, "Guns are like other things in life. Some are for looking at and some are for using. But if you would use one of my 'for show' guns, I would never get upset. Why, if you confused a gun for shooting and a gun for showing, it would be no big deal. Now, if you will excuse me, I just cleaned a gun and I need to wash my hands and dry them on my pants."

RUNNING THE RIGHT OFF-GAME

My little Rebel dog has quite a reputation for hunting birds. I am not bragging but I know that I kill more birds than many bird hunters I have talked to. The reason I am not bragging, is because I am in the woods more than they are, and I shoot more ammunition than they do. My little Rebel might flush a dozen or more grouse before I get one. He might flush a score of woodcock before one falls, which means he only has to flush 200 in order for me to get a meal. Pheasant he does much better on and will often circle them back to me on the ground before they flush, and once the pheasant do flush they are much more ponderous and easier to draw a bead on.

Well, I may not brag on the number of birds in the bag, but I do brag on my dog's eagerness to help the kitchen table with a few birds. This is what led me to taking a local grouse hunter, Jimbo, hunting with my beagle. He mocked my dog's ability on birds and ridiculed his success rate. So, we made a friendly wager; Reb and I could get more variety of game in one day than Jimbo could with his shorthair.

The morning started slow and by that I mean it started with a 40 minute rabbit chase. It took that long to shoot the rabbit. The bunny circled three circles before I saw it and then I was able to get the rabbit in the vest. The unfortunate part of the chase was that it hurt my competition because I was there looking for birds. After the rabbit chase Reb started getting a happy tail again but not barking, which is a good giveaway that he is on a bird. I was really running to keep up with the dog. Reb works a bird line much more aggressively than a trained bird dog. Jimbo was behind me as we climbed the hill. The grouse flushed and we heard it go out, but never saw the thing. We had just double-timed up a long, steep hill for no shot.

"What...are you doing?" Jimbo gasped.

"Hunting...grouse...why?" I replied, equally out of breath.

"Oh...my...God...you're nuts."

Just then, Reb jumped another rabbit. "Don't worry... Jimbo," I said, "You...can catch your breath while Reb runs this rabbit" A half-hour later the rabbit either ran in a hole or my dog lost it. I don't believe my Reb loses too many rabbits, but I wouldn't be so bold as a lot of guys who claim that it never happens. I can tell you this, there is no way I was going into the briars where he lost the rabbit to determine if Mr. Bunny went subterranean or if Reb failed.

I can only describe the next hour as a barrage of noise. Reb flushed grouse. I saw a few and I shot at them, nothing that brought success. When a grouse flushes in thickets and saplings it is pretty hard for anybody. It is especially hard when your bird dog is a tri-color beagle running a bird mute with the same intensity as he would pound a rabbit. Many times I just couldn't get close enough to shoot. Many other times I shot while trying to catch my breath. If you want to make some money, buy stock in ammunition companies when I am hunting birds with my beagle.

Jimbo was feeling pretty smug when Reb flushed a grouse out into an open clearing between the thickets and a pond. I saw the bird early and it flew straight as an arrow —a shot that anybody could make, even a winded guy fighting for air while chasing a beagle for grouse. Add a grouse to the bag. Time to water the dog and head out to a new location. Do you remember how Batman always put a blindfold on people he took into the Bat Cave? Jimbo got a blindfold as I bounced my '78 Land Cruiser into a spot that I wasn't about to share with this bird boy. Off with the blindfold.

"Let's go Jimbo," I said.

"Impress me," He dared.

We were hunting right along a prime woodcock flight. I knew that the birds went through there every year. It was the reason I bought a migratory game bird stamp each season. Jim got nervous when he saw me pause before I let Reb out and put on a pair of sneakers and Filson chaps. I don't know how far we ran following Reb. I do know how many rounds I fired—it was in the double digits. When I finally killed a woodcock, Jimbo was at the bottom of a hill a quarter mile behind me sucking wind. The truth is that there are so many woodcock in that area that one could probably get one without a dog. A good shooter with a close bird dog could do great. That is why I didn't want Jim to know where I was. Reb ran a rabbit and I managed to get an easy shot on it. Add another bunny.

I changed my sneakers and put dry socks on (lots of mud in that woodcock spot). Off to another spot. If I could get a pheasant, I would be confident that Jim would not touch me with his shorthair; not because his shorthair isn't great, it is, but I know more spots to hunt than he does. We drove to a farm that is close to a place where the game commission will stock pheasant that tend to stay flocked up together for weeks.

The pheasant hunt started bad, which means another good rabbit run. The chase ended with another dead rabbit and was followed by another roaring rabbit chase. That second chase ended up in woodchuck heaven. It is a small hilltop with lots of woodchuck holes and no woodchucks. Lots of people claim that the coyote can kill woodchucks easily and that chuck-less holes often mean that the woodchucks/groundhogs have been eaten by the 'yotes. Which is why I call that hill woodchuck heaven. I was sure that the rabbit holed. "Well, my little dog lost another one Jimbo," I explained, "Oh well. I'm sure your dog will run rabbits better."

It was getting late in the afternoon when Reb started clucking like a chicken. He does this on pheasant. It is the same noise he makes when he starts a rabbit, sometimes. But he will cluck for an entire circle on a pheasant. And the pheasant will circle like a cottontail. Reb was moving through a small stand of mostly harvested field corn towards a pasture. I ran to keep up. At the end of the corn field, just at the edge of the stalks, three hen pheasant flushed (it is legal to shoot hens in much of PA). I stopped running, tried to control my breathing, and looked at the three birds. The first one flushed too far to my right, I missed the second one, and the third one fell as I shot. I reloaded and Reb stuck his head in the air and walked into the corn field 30 yards to my left. Another hen flushed and it hovered after the first shot and fell on the second.

I decided to let Reb hunt for one more rabbit. He chased a rabbit that I saw sneak by me and I couldn't shoot it because all I saw was the hind end. The chase ended at a tree. We can call it a loss if Jim feels better. As Reb circled wider looking for fresh rabbit scent, a gray squirrel ran up a tree and I shot it.

"Jim," I said, "Three rabbits, a grouse, a woodcock, two pheasants, and a squirrel ain't bad."

"Yeah, I thought you were nuts letting him run all those rabbits all that time. You only needed one rabbit. The goal was to get the most variety."

"Sure, but that ain't our style. Reb and I hunt rabbits and if a bird is available we take the shot. I may have hunted more spots than I typically would today in order to get variety. But all of the spots we hunted are places that I hunt rabbits. I would never pull him off a rabbit to look for a bird."

You may ask me about Jimbo's shorthair; it is a great dog. He managed to bring home a limit of grouse and a limit of pheasant. We didn't get out of breath either. Jimbo did it in less ammunition than I did too. Glory be, the dog even flushed a rabbit that Jimbo managed to miss on the jump. "Stay put, Jim. The dog will circle it back." I said. Jim sneered at me. His shorthair is better on birds than my beagle is on rabbits. But don't tell him that.

Ah, and Jimbo will tell people about the day my little beagle was a bird dog. Truth is, he isn't that great on birds. Reality is that I spend a lot of time looking for rabbits and in the process find lots of birds. The embarrassing part is that my little Reb will even get happy-tailed on sparrows once in a while—*shh*, it's a secret. Truth is that I shoot more birds flushing as Reb chases rabbits and makes noise than I do birds that Reb is actively working. But don't tell Jimbo, he's busy trying to teach his shorthair to hark in. What do you do with three rabbits, two pheasant, one grouse, one woodcock, and one squirrel? Chili. I love chili, it has a little of this and a little of that; which is how Reb and I hunt.

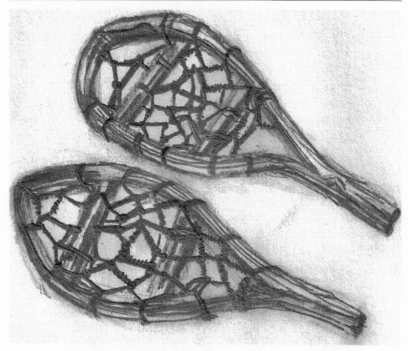

Snowy Sanctuary

I do not want to sound disapproving but there just seems to be something terribly sensational about getting snow related forecasts from The Weather Channel. In part, I think this may be due to the fact that The Weather Channel is based out of Georgia. I mean a skiff of snow paralyzes that place and so forecasts of a few inches seem dreadful. It is akin to my hearing a forecast for Pennsylvania for 90+ degree temperatures with high humidity in the summer—I panic and wonder how I can possibly get by in those conditions. By contrast, many southerners would simply shrug that forecast off as being not very threatening.

Growing up in the northwestern part of PA, I thought that 3 inches of snow was called a standard morning.

Many nights the air came off Lake Erie and deposited a fresh several inches of snow. Such flurries did not even make the news forecast, it was just presumed that when the sun set in the evenings and the air cooled as it rose over the Allegheny Plateau. The end result would be a few inches of snow. That was winter. School wasn't delayed, no public service announcements scrolled on the television, and no one panicked. Things appear to be different now. I have even noticed that school will be delayed because it is cold outside; although, I haven't seen the real value of delaying school for two hours while the temperature rises from -15 degrees to -11, as if the 4 degrees made all the difference. Besides, most kids sit in an idling car with their mothers waiting for the bus to appear. We were told not to worry about how cold it was because we would be walking to school and that would keep us warm.

And then there is all the fuss in the grocery stores in advance of a forecast of a few inches of snow. Suddenly everyone feels a need to buy milk, bread, and 6 rolls of toilet paper. I'm sorry, but if milk and bread affect your gastrointestinal system in such a negative fashion as to require that much toilet paper usage over a day or two, then maybe you should reconsider what ingredients ought to comprise your emergency diet. I see carts loaded with several loaves of bread and gallons of milk. They could live on toast soaked in milk and not use it all before it spoiled!

At first I thought that I was being too severe on people for being so sensational about the fact that it does indeed snow in the winter, but I am not alone in this cynicism. I have been talking to school teachers, and they agree that the fear of winter has reached a feverish pitch that is not warranted. As one teacher said, "Two hour delays are bad enough—the kids aren't in school long enough to learn but a cancellation for no good reason results in school lasting well into summer and June is not conducive to learning for kids!" The same teacher also feels that the routine snowfalls of previous decades are now perceived as events that cripple entire towns.

I have spent the entire second rabbit season living in solidarity with our educators. When school is delayed or cancelled, I too take the same hours off work. I have had a great winter rabbit season. The dogs are running well and I have always loved the second season for hunting those woods rabbits that tend to run the timber. The fresh powder makes it easy to identify the quarry by looking at the tracks, because isn't it peculiar how an old woods grey rabbit will run oh so similar to a deer? Oh, and I have refused to live on milk and bread! That is only a milk beverage substitution better than the despised traditional fare of prisoners (although if you have done any prison ministry you will find that prisoners eat much better today!). No sir, when the flakes fall I like to blast a few bunnies and then feast on rabbit pot pie, or rabbit fajitas, or deboned rabbit slow cooked into a sandwich that many would swear to be pulled pork. Baked beans and coleslaw help the afternoon just fine. An evening in front of the fireplace cleaning a shotgun with the smell of Hoppe's in my nose and the snore of tired beagles in my ears is an ideal blizzard to me.

The last big blast of winter (about 4 inches of snow was all) found me in the grocery store the night before, navigating the blitz of people scrounging for milk and bread. I bought some really expensive aged cheddar cheese, some soda pop, and the vegetables to make homemade venison and rabbit chili. I also purchased some pig ear dog treats anticipating a good day afield. Winter is a joy for us beaglers. I know of no better way to locate new rabbit cover than a beautiful, fresh blanket of snow. By March the air will soon be warming up. I love winter and hate to see it go. March might yet yield some snow, and if it does, I will be eagerly bounding through the thickets looking for rabbit tracks in the powder. The hot air of summer will be here soon enough and I will groan and complain about the heat that will have its hot hand on our necks. August is a month that I would gladly trade for another winter month, but who am I to complain? And if I did complain about hot temperatures in August, do you think the people in Georgia would laugh at me?

Oh well, let the world fear the potential of March snowflakes. My refrigerator is stocked with cheese and a few cans of cola for a late snack. The freezer has homemade bratwursts made from wild game and the cupboard has some sauerkraut for cooking them. Hidden high on top of the freezer is a bag of pig ears for the beagles. The Weather Channel may have convinced most northerners to see snow and run for cover and live on bread and milk, but I for one, see the winter storms as an opportunity to have a nice hunt afield and then retreat to a snowy sanctuary for a relaxing evening of reading as the beagles curl into balls at my feet and dream of check free chases.

SWEETER 16

I shoot a lot of rabbits, more than most people. Numbers aren't everything but under 50 rabbits is a bad year for me. That being said, I will also add a few facts. One fact is that it takes good dogs to get that many rabbits —not great dogs necessarily—but good ones. It also takes lots of time in the brush and briars. I hunt every day of the season. I hunt all day on Saturdays and a couple hours each day on Monday through Friday. Trust me, I am not bragging, a better shot than me with better dogs than mine could probably stack up many more rabbits if he knew the locales that I do.

So, I am in the woods a lot. Running beagles and hunting rabbits is my means of relaxing and also my greatest sport. It would stand to reason that this requires me to have a gun that suits me. I have always wanted a nice side-by-side 16 gauge, a Fox preferably, but I would settle for a regular 'ol Stevens or an Ithaca. My father had a Fox in the 1950's. He lost the fore stock of it in the field and rather than worry about finding replacement parts, he sold it and used a different shotgun. He was raising 5 kids at the time. Later on, Dad raised my sister and I. He never cared much about what gun he used, but he spoke fondly of that old Fox 16 gauge he had in the 1950's.

I suppose I have always spent too much on my hunting equipment. When I was sixteen years old, I had a job working for the Allegheny National Forest; nothing grand, teenagers helping out with manual labor for $3.35/hour. I spent my entire first week's pay on a pair of leather boots. This is when things like Gore-Tex and Thinsulate were relatively new technology. I wore those boots hard and still got seven years out of them. In other words, I own good gear and sit on worthless furniture. I stay high, dry and warm in all weather and have never owned anything near a new vehicle. I own enough pairs of boots that I would have to stop typing right now to count the exact number if I really wanted to relate the statistic to you, and the computer at which I sit is an outdated hand-me-down. I own good hounds that I bought from good breeders but I have the most basic cable package available on the T.V set. My beagles eat one of the more expensive flavors of *Purina* available and I plant a big garden for myself. You get the point: I love the outdoors as much as you do.

So, out of a borrowed nostalgia, I have been looking for a Fox 16. It is a nostalgia that was my dad's, but I have taken it upon myself to find the gun that he had to sell. O.K., maybe not *the* gun, but one much like it. Well, I found one. Built in Philadelphia in 1928. Is it rare? A little. Expensive? No. It's used; a good bit used but still very functional. It's a nice little Fox Sterlingworth, bored improved and modified. I brought it home and I put it with my pump action, Ithaca 16 gauge which is the gun that Dad used while he and I hunted together.

I can hear some now. Why a 16? I guess as a tribute to another time. Many still talk about the Browning Sweet 16. For me this Fox is a sweeter 16. It's light too; mounted on a 20-gauge frame. I know, today's 12 gauges are lighter than a 16 and have more punch. I also know that modern loads in a 20 are every bit as potent as a 16. I don't care.

One of the reasons I shoot as many rabbits as I do is because I do not take every shot that comes by. I only shoot the ones I can make. Some days I go home with an empty vest and it is all right with me. I like to think of times gone by that I missed. Days with 16 gauges being common, farms abundant and four lane highways fewer. Days with guns made with more care. Guns made with wood. Wood that scratches and nicks and splinters to add character. Guns that people kept for a lifetime rather than swapping every season for a new fad. Oh, I know full well how well the new shotguns perform. A plastic stocked camouflage shotgun made brand new today is very effective. I can tell you about many times where I took hunters out for their first rabbit hunts. Out they come, 12 gauge autoloader in hand, synthetic stock, big powder and big shot. They laughed at my little 16 Ithaca, "What are you gonna do with that little 2 3/4" shell with number 7 shot?" They would cry.

"Shoot rabbits."

"What will you do when it runs by at 45 yards?" they chided more.

"Wait for the next circle, enjoy the chase, and see if the rabbit gets closer."

Blank stares would meet my words. Everything today is about larger shells, more powder, more lead, longer shots. As far as I am concerned, a nice vintage gun ought to be a sign of professionalism. Like using wooden bats in major league baseball. A good athlete can still get the job done.

Sadly, the craze today is for more velocity and more lead. It is almost as if we are substituting raw fire power in the place of learning and instead of understanding the game species we hunt. Half the fun of rabbit hunting is learning the escape routes and finding the holes, and discovering where to stand, and where to expect shots. It is not a tragedy to not shoot, it allows us to come back tomorrow to chase again.

"I killed a rabbit at almost 60 yards." A guy once told me.

"Good Lord man, why?" I replied.

"I had 3" high brass loads in my 12 gauge and thought I would end the chase before the rabbit holed." I shook my head wondering how many rabbits he wounded that way only to die in a hole later.

The worst example I can think of in terms of overpowering the game we pursue was a rabbit hunter I talked with in one of our many reclaimed strip mines here in PA. I knew the fellow, which is to say that I knew his name and where he lives, and I know that his dogs spend 350 days each year on their chains in the yard. He was shooting rabbits on the jump because his hounds couldn't circle a rabbit-probably from lack of exercise. He had an autoloader, 3" shells, and bandoleers. I am not exaggerating in the slightest when I tell you that he looked like Pancho Villa. He must have been carrying 4 boxes of ammunition across his chest and around his waist. I was looking over my shoulder for the *Federalis*. Strapped on "Pancho's" hip was a long dagger, presumably to field dress the rabbits and to extract the buckshot out of the flesh. Backing up the desperado was his gang of bandits, all laden with copious quantities of ammunition and wielding autoloaders. One was wearing face paint—and he wasn't hunting turkey or bow hunting deer!

I stood in awe beside Pancho, careful to keep my hound on leash. I had a little .410 with me that day. Every once in a while, when I expect to get long chases, I take the little gun with me intending to shoot no more than 20 yards. Behind the gang was a vast pile of ejected, empty cartridges. Scattered around the brush were other such piles of empty cartridges.

"They're in here but they go in the hole quick," The face painted warrior spoke.

"No they don't," I said, "They run good here, that's why I brought my little .410." Just then a hound tongued, a rabbit burst out of a thicket, a barrage of artillery went off at a target over 50 yards away and the rabbit kept going. Behind that firing squad a new puddle of plastic and brass cartridges formed. The dogs quit barking as suddenly as they started.

"Went in the hole," Pancho spit out some tobacco.

"Ah, bull," I said, "I'll let my dog loose on that rabbit and no one shoots this rabbit but me." The dog ran over, grabbed the line and moved out. One circle was made with Pancho's dogs harking in for some of the run. I never saw the rabbit go by. The second circle was bigger, much bigger. The rabbit came by and stood 10 yards from me. I waved my hands at the rabbit and watched it run off down a shallow ravine. The crowd couldn't believe that I didn't shoot the cottontail. I picked up my dog when he came by and Pancho's hounds lost the line.

"I suppose that one went in a hole too?" I asked.

Pancho reared up, "You think you got a hot shot dog or something?"

"Nope. Just an average one, maybe a little better than average because he eats rabbit tracks 3 days each week most of the year, even if just for an hour at a time. I'll come back and hunt some other day. Police your brass if you don't mind, those empty shells look like hell."

There is no reason why a shotgun can't be effective, efficient, and artistic. I don't want a molded stock. I don't want a camouflage shotgun. I don't want a shot pattern that requires me to eat my rabbits with extreme trepidation, waiting for a hard crunch as BB and molar do the grind. I yearned for years for a sweeter 16, the gun my dad spoke so fondly about, the gun that I had never even fired.

So, after a 4 or 5 year search, I found the gun I have wanted for so long, at a price that was affordable. American Steel, with American wood, and American craftsmanship built right here in my home state. Now for the kicker: it is chambered 2 9/16". I can't use a 3" shell, which does not bother me. However, I can't even use a standard 2 3/4" shell. Immediately, half of my friends tried to talk me into rechambering the gun to 2 3/4".

"Ford," they all told me, "I know a gunsmith who can make that gun right for ya." I resisted. The gun was already "right" and I decided to find some 2 1/2" shells to fit it rather than drag my new Sterlingworth into an era it did not belong. I wanted to go back to the era of the Fox, not drag the Fox to the era of Pancho.

The rest of my friends all wanted me to put the gun on the wall, "Just show it. It is too nice to shoot. Someday it will really be worth something."

"Yeah, yeah," I would sigh to those friends, "But who cares what it will be worth *someday*. Especially since I never plan to sell it."

"What if it gets scratched or something?"

"I would rather look back at that gun someday with memories of rabbits and hounds and hunts and special days. I don't want to look at it and think of how it looked on a wall."

I began an investigation for ammo for my Fox. Wow! What a search. I called, looked and hunted. I tried the internet and found a few companies who sold them. One sporting good store told me that they had a source but that it was dreadfully difficult to get the ammunition into the states; it was hard to import from Europe because of the restrictions in this post 9/11 world. What a joke. I can't imagine a terrorist wanting to use a shotgun over a more potent weapon, and even if they did, why would they wait for imported boxes of lower powder, shorter rounds when big 3"+ rounds could be obtained from any department store?

I needed a better jump dog to find these shells. I put my editors, Bob and Pearl Baker on the job. Bob looked and hunted and got back to me. "Did you try Lion Country Supply? It's right down the road from you"

"No," I confessed, "I tried Grice's, right up the road. I think they are the largest gun store in the state."

"Yeah," Bob said, "But Lion Country sells a lot of imported guns and some of those are chambered for 2 1/2" shells. I called them, and sure enough, just over the hill, and along the valley, at Lion Country Supply, just as Bob predicted, I found some shells. The Polywad Corporation, in Macon, Georgia, made these shells; there is a supplier in the country! The shells were a spreader load, or Spred-R, as the Polywad Corporation markets their loads. Spreader loads were once more common and hunters I have talked to have fond memories of their effectiveness on rabbits, their patterns widening out quicker and more fully—perfect for shooting at bouncing blurs of fur.

I couldn't wait to shoot the gun. I called Fred, "I just found shells for that Fox, wanna go shoot?"

"Yeah, stop by and we'll go out back."

"We put some paint on some cardboard and proceeded to pattern the gun. Wow! The four feet square piece of cardboard was utterly covered at 35 yards with the 7 1/2 shot. Ditto for the 6 shot. I was extremely impressed. We decided to shoot a few more rounds. Fred didn't have any clay targets, so he threw some cans out for me to shoot. At any and all ranges the Spred-R loads were just awesome. They are a great blend of old fashioned craftsmanship and some new-fangled technology.

"One last throw?" Fred asked.

"Sure."

"I'll stand behind you and throw it right in front of you. A falling target no more than two feet in front of you. Hard shot, you ready?"

"Yeah. Let's do it" I nodded.

"Wanna make it interesting?" Fred coaxed, "If you can hit it no more than two feet away from you, I will buy you a Pepsi." Fred knows my cold beverage of choice.

"Fine," I said, "go ahead and throw it."

The can arched up and over my head. It was falling fast and would be hard to time. I tracked the can with the bead. I began with the gun pointed high almost above me. I traced it lower and finally when at shoulder height I let the gun simply rest gently in the crook of my arm. The can landed with a soft 'ping' sound as aluminum and grass met about eighteen inches in front of me. I pointed the Fox at the resting can and blasted it. Fred stared in shock. He never said the can had to be less than two feet away and *still* moving.

"How far away from me was it when I shot it Fred?" I smiled, "Less than two feet?"

"You no-good whelped dog," Fred said, only he phrased it different than that.

I laughed and Fred laughed too as we walked off for my soda pop, "I like that new Vanilla Pepsi," I instigated.

I emailed and called Polywad and soon received some other shells to sample in the 16-gauge (chambered for 2 1/2" guns). They sent me two different types of shells besides the famous Spred-R loads. They are called the Vintager and the Doublewides. These loads are available by calling the company and they are designed to be a little more economical than the Spred-R. I was impressed with these rounds as well. Polywad makes all of these great products in a wide range of gauges, lengths, shot sizes, and powder loads. Whatever your gun, they can sell you a great product. Oh, dig out your old guns and give me a call. We'll go out and frustrate the Pancho Villa's of rabbit hunting. We'll run and gun for fun. We'll let some get away and we'll really be pleased with the ones we do shoot. And when we eat our rabbits we won't have to chew with fear as we wait for a BB to lodge itself into a filling in our teeth. Just don't make a wager with me over Pepsi; us United Methodists aren't allowed to gamble. Pepsi is a sweet drink with a sweeter 16.

Made in the USA
Charleston, SC
04 January 2012